Louis XIV

in Historical Thought

Historical Controversies · A Norton Series

Under the general editorship of BRYCE LYON, *Brown University*

This series has been developed in response to the growing interest in historical interpretation, in the how and why of history as opposed to pure narrative accounts. Each volume discusses a major historical problem with analysis of the leading interpretations past and present.

THE ORIGINS OF THE MIDDLE AGES • Bryce Lyon
THE KING'S PARLIAMENT OF ENGLAND • George O. Sayles
LOUIS XIV IN HISTORICAL THOUGHT • William F. Church

Louis XIV

in Historical Thought

FROM VOLTAIRE TO THE ANNALES SCHOOL

by William F. Church

Brown University

W · W · Norton & Company, Inc · New York

FIRST EDITION

Copyright © 1976 by W. W. Norton & Company, Inc. All Rights Reserved.
Published simultaneously in Canada by George J. McLeod Limited,
Toronto. Printed in the United States of America.

Library of Congress Cataloging in Publication Data
Church, William Farr, 1912–
    Louis XIV in historical thought from Voltaire to the Annales school.
    1. France—History—Louis XIV, 1643–1715—Historiography. 2. Louis
XIV, King of France, 1638–1715.
I. Title.
DC126.C44   1976   944'.033'072   75–30574
ISBN 0–393–05563–9
ISBN 0–393–09211–9 pbk.

1 2 3 4 5 6 7 8 9

Contents

Introduction

The idea that certain historical periods are genuinely "great" ages has been both fruitful and frustrating to those who have attempted to trace the growth of western culture. Although historians from Thucydides to Toynbee have been fascinated by the rise and fall of civilizations, much remains to be discovered concerning the dynamics that produce such phenomena in human affairs. There is, nevertheless, a general consensus that a limited number of periods may be characterized as truly great ages, and that they were unusually significant not only because of their achievements in their own time but also because of their contributions to the growth of western civilization. The exceptional nature of these eras has been investigated by innumerable historians who have sought to identify their outstanding features in time and place, yet these same periods can also be shown to have possessed qualities of universal significance in any age. For this reason they were invariably highly self-conscious and very aware of their own greatness.

This was apparent during the "age of Louis XIV," to borrow Voltaire's famous phrase. Indeed, one of the major characteristics of the period was the conviction of contemporaries that they were living in momentous times, and they made extensive efforts to preserve the memory of their era for the edification of posterity. More than any other European people, the French compiled voluminous memoirs of their personal experiences, creating a literature that provides invaluable insights into the mentality of the age. As the chief actor in the drama, Louis XIV

sought to perpetuate the record of his achievements by establishing archives of official documents and commissioning histories of his reign. Likewise many lesser participants, such as officeholders, jurists, clerics, military men, and the like, recorded
their accomplishments and frequently assembled family archives of correspondence and other materials. Colbert reflected
the prevailing mood when, in justification of his policies, he
wrote to his royal master in 1669: "Bear in mind that we are not
in an era of small things." And in retrospect we must agree that
the reign of the Sun King was of momentous significance to the
fortunes of Europe and the development of its civilization.

There was, furthermore, general recognition of the fact that
France owed much of her greatness to her monarchy because it
provided the leadership that was indispensable to national revival. Not only was the monarchy the focal point of French patriotism; all observers knew that it had restored order to France
after she had been torn apart by religious division, social fragmentation, economic dislocation, intense factionalism, and divided loyalties during the Wars of Religion and through much
of the bureaucracy creation of a permanent military establish-
narchical leadership took the form of massive, authoritarian
state-building by the French kings and their ministers. So comprehensive was their effort that it included not only expansion
of the bureaucracy, creation of a permanent military establishment, economic regulation, and territorial expansion, but also
the channeling of French talent in intellectual and cultural pursuits. The monarchy provided the framework and much of the
impetus for the dynamic elements of the age that were most
noticed by contemporaries and was correspondingly idealized.

Within Louis XIV's very long reign (1643–1715), the first
generation of his personal rule, from 1661 to approximately
1685, was the period of greatest brilliance and success of absolute monarchy. This was due in part to fortuitous and extremely
favorable circumstances, since all factors, foreign and domestic,
combined to place maximum power in Louis XIV's hands immediately upon his assumption of control. At home the general
acceptance of divine-right absolutism was so pervasive that it
was held to be the only viable and rightful form of government,
while abroad no power or combination of powers presented any

challenge to French supremacy. A series of expert ministers, of whom Colbert and Louvois were but the ablest, carried the work of state-building forward on many fronts and greatly increased the effective power of the sovereign. All Europe was dazzled by the building of Versailles and its brilliant court, which was graced by the presence of the greatest French nobles and other luminaries. The court of Versailles set the standard for all other courts, and French literature, drama, the arts, and the language itself attained a perfection previously unknown, in part under royal patronage. The achievements of French culture both equaled and enhanced the splendor of the Grand Monarch, who became the arbiter of Europe's affairs and succeeded in raising the prestige of the Bourbons to unprecedented heights. French was the language of diplomacy, and Louis XIV's diplomats and generals were superior to all others. The wars in which Louis XIV engaged were as much for the purpose of increasing his personal prestige and renown as anything else, and brought added glory to the ruler, the Bourbon dynasty, and the nation. Even popular uprisings, so constant earlier in the century, gradually dwindled. Under such circumstances, it is not surprising that contemporaries were entirely laudatory of the regime, its policies, and its monarch. For a rare moment both the ideology and the practices of absolutism won general acceptance. To many observers it seemed that the centuries of effort by the French kings to increase their power and achieve supremacy in Europe's affairs had attained their true fruition.

This relatively felicitous historical moment, however, did not last more than approximately a single generation. As the reign progressed, the problems of government became more acute, the quality of personnel declined in all fields, and Louis XIV's policies began to take their toll. These changes were slow to appear and did not fundamentally alter the stature of the Grand Monarch or French hegemony in Europe, yet there were increasing evidences that his rule was becoming more burdensome and arbitrary. Extensive trouble was experienced with the Jansenists and the Huguenots. The former were condemned and dispersed, while the latter were outlawed by the revocation of the Edict of Nantes with important losses to the realm and major international repercussions. The royal administration

suppressed many local liberties and relentlessly exploited the
human and material resources of the realm to support the
chronic warfare in which Louis XIV engaged. Continual war
was undoubtedly the major cause of disruption, since it led to
tightened controls over the mass of the population, required
increased taxation and a host of questionable fiscal expedients,
and caused widespread economic decline and even depopulation. Louis XIV's wars pitted France against almost all Europe,
were increasingly adverse to French interests, and were punctuated by disastrous defeats on the field of battle. The confidence of the first generation was replaced by hostility and
questioning even by many who stood high in the social hierarchy and were beneficiaries of the regime. Such outstanding
observers as Marshal Vauban, the Duc de Saint-Simon, the
Comte de Boulainvilliers, and Archbishop Fénelon severely
criticized Louis XIV's policies as contrary to the good of the
nation, and massive decline on many fronts confirmed their
fears. Their strictures, however, were directed toward Louis
XIV's policies rather than his stature and renown, which survived substantially intact even in defeat. In fact, his critics were
indirectly paying tribute to the enormous import of his rule by
expressing their great concern. And all agreed that the reign of
the Sun King, for better or worse, would long be remembered
by posterity.

   These reactions to Louis XIV's rule clearly indicate both the
advantages and the disadvantages of contemporary observers
when they attempted to estimate the significance of events in
their own time. Their advantages were many in that they lived
through and often witnessed important events, were aware of
a thousand ephemeral circumstances that are impossible to re-
capture, and experienced firsthand the psychology of the Age
of Absolutism. On the other hand, they lacked the breadth of
information, perspectives, methodology, and other assets of
later historians. The latter soon made their appearance and initiated their massive work of reevaluation, for within a generation after Louis XIV's death Voltaire composed his memorable
synthesis, the first comprehensive exposition of the greatness of
the "age of Louis XIV." Voltaire not only viewed the reign as
one of the four great ages of western history; he interpreted it

as the greatest of the four, literally the heir to the ages. And subsequent to Voltaire the reign has attracted the attention of many of France's ablest historians. Their personal viewpoints have often been utterly opposed to much that was fundamental to Louis XIV's reign—absolutism, social inequality, religious intolerance, even classicism in letters and the arts—but they never denied its historical significance. This, however, they re-interpreted in a variety of ways. By discovering new information, developing new techniques of research, and, above all, by introducing new perspectives, they have extensively rectified the historical record and added to our understanding of this period, which was undeniably one of the most momentous in all French history. Most important, they carefully weighed and evaluated the innumerable elements of Louis XIV's reign in an effort to determine whether it was in any sense a great period in the growth of western civilization. The evolution of their views is the subject of this study.

Finally, a word of caution. This short volume is not meant to cover all elements of Louis XIV's long and extremely significant reign. Neither is it intended as a guide to a complete bibliography of Louis XIV. These are available elsewhere. My intention is merely to show the major trends in the growth of knowledge of Louis XIV and the corresponding interpretations of his place in history. Only those works that bear directly upon this very large subject and are illustrative of the main currents of historical interpretation are considered here. References to many are brief and incomplete in the text; complete information on all will be found in the appended Bibliography.

1. Voltaire's Synthesis

Although Louis XIV avidly desired to perpetuate the memory of his greatness, no outstanding historical account of his achievements appeared during or immediately after his reign. This reflected the fact that the Age of Absolutism was anything but congenial to the writing of history with any degree of objectivity. The period had all the qualities of an ideological age in which the traditions, rights, privileges, and conceptual framework of the monarchy not only were generally accepted but were also revered as sacred. Its powers and policies were therefore not to be questioned, for to do so was to fly in the face of divine decree. Conformity to the official position by historians was ensured both by the pressure of public opinion and by the system of censorship, which required all printers to submit two copies of all publications for examination by the royal censors. In this context any examination of royal policy risked offending the great by the simple process of analyzing state secrets. The result was that only laudatory histories were published in France, and the few historians who criticized Louis XIV wrote from abroad.

True, the period was far from devoid of historical scholarship. The most active group was the Benedictine Congregation of St. Maur. These dedicated and extremely prolific men developed new techniques of historical investigation and produced a phenomenal body of publications, but they essentially limited

their efforts to editing records and earlier tracts, and scrupulously refrained from touching on the reign of the Sun King.
The result was a thoroughgoing divorce of near-contemporary
history and historical erudition. The most successful historians
during Louis XIV's reign were Mézeray at its beginning and
Father Daniel at its end, but both prudently terminated their
works with the assassination of Henry IV in 1610. Even so, Mézeray's account of earlier kings' policies relative to taxation
aroused the ire of Colbert, who caused Mézeray's pension from
the crown to be suppressed. Father Daniel protected himself
with an ultra-laudatory dedicatory preface to Louis XIV.

Meanwhile, Louis XIV sought to promote the writing of an
official history of his reign, but the results were meager indeed.
The most important work was that of the royal historiographer,
Paul Pellisson. His *Histoire de Louis XIV* relates events from
1661 to 1678 but was not published until 1749. Pellisson also
cooperated in compiling the king's memoirs, but these remained
in very fragmentary condition. The Academy of Inscriptions
and Medals issued its sumptuous *Histoire métallique* of Louis
XIV, but this merely reproduced and described the medals that
had been struck to commemorate great state occasions. On the
other hand, the latter part of the reign witnessed the appearance in Amsterdam of Michel Levassor's multi-volume *Histoire
du règne de Louis XIII*. A Calvinist in exile, Levassor wrote for
the purpose of excoriating French absolutism and all that it represented. His preface denounces Louis XIV's rule as vainglori-
ous, exploitive, and tyrannical to the point of extinguishing the
last spark of liberty in France. The works of Pellisson and Levassor vividly demonstrate the inability of contemporary historians to dissociate themselves from *a priori* viewpoints.

Louis XIV's death in 1715 lessened official pressures for conformity, but this did not immediately produce any important
history of the reign. The Abbé de Saint-Pierre and the Duc de
Saint-Simon compiled critical commentaries on Louis XIV's
policies, but these contain little more than highly partisan, personalized observations. Saint-Pierre's *Annales politiques* argues
that a ruler may be considered great only if he ameliorates the
human condition, and he consequently found much to condemn
in Louis XIV's rule. Saint-Simon composed his *Parallèle des*

trois premiers rois Bourbons for the express purpose of rehabilitating the reputation of Louis XIII, whose personal conduct and official policies he found superior to those of the Sun King in every essential. In the interim, the more formal histories of Louis XIV by Limiers, Larrey, and Avrigny had been published. These contain a mountain of specifics but present no broader interpretation of even the more salient features of the reign. Clearly, the field needed the hand of a master to give it new direction and perspective.

VOLTAIRE'S VIEW OF LOUIS XIV AND HIS AGE

It was in this situation that Voltaire made his momentous contribution with his *Siècle de Louis XIV*. Although the major thrust of the Enlightenment ran counter to much that the Sun King stood for, the movement nevertheless produced one of his greatest historian champions of all time. Rejecting the theological view of history that Bossuet had so extensively developed in his *Discours sur l'histoire universelle,* Voltaire brought history down to earth and attempted to view it in essentially human terms. Human nature he held to be constant in all ages, but accrued "ways" (*mœurs*) not only varied greatly among peoples but were also the essence of human experience, culture, and achievement, and were therefore the proper subject of history. Only by examining all elements of a civilization —customs, laws, manners, institutions, economy, society, arts, letters, philosophy, and religion, as well as great movements and the contributions of leaders—might the historian understand the essential spirit of a people and the changes that occurred in its mentality over the ages. These principles he applied most extensively in his epoch-making *Essai sur les mœurs et l'esprit des nations.*

Voltaire's most successful historical study was his *Siècle de Louis XIV*. Its subject was thoroughly congenial to him because he had spent his youth in the France that had been produced by Louis XIV's reign and instinctively admired much that it represented, including the monarch himself. A product of two decades of intermittent but painstaking research, the work is based upon careful analysis of a mass of sources, including much unpublished material. This he used with great discrimination, since mere factual reportage was the furthest from his intentions. Instead he sought to select and present those elements that would elucidate the civilization and spirit of the age. For this reason he made extensive use of the materials of cultural and intellectual history, treating them in his novel and highly subjective fashion.

Voltaire's stated reason for portraying the period of Louis XIV in this manner was his conviction that it constituted one of the few genuinely great ages of western civilization. The others, for him, had occurred in Periclean Athens, Augustan Rome, and Italy during the Renaissance. In Voltaire's view all these historical moments—and only these—had witnessed perfection in the arts and letters and greatness of the human mind. Recognizing that their achievements had not been equal in all fields, Voltaire persuaded himself that the age of Louis XIV was the greatest of all, largely because of the growth of rational philosophy. Voltaire's criterion of historical greatness was therefore one of cultural climax, as represented by achievements in the higher elements of civilization, especially in the realm of the mind. The latter he found the key to the greatness of France under Louis XIV and the reason for her superiority. With this approach, it is not surprising that he produced a novel and laudatory account of the period.

Voltaire realized, however, that the cultural attainments of any age depend upon a host of factors other than the intellectual and can be understood only in their broader historical context. He therefore found it necessary to analyze a wide variety of topics and to include much "traditional" history despite his claim to present only what is essential to a man of taste. After describing the condition of France before 1661, emphasizing the miseries of the Fronde and Mazarin's ineptitudes, Voltaire devotes approximately half of his volume to foreign affairs, chiefly military and to a lesser extent diplomatic. These chapters are by far the most tedious in the book and contain extensive accounts of sieges and battles—precisely the type of information that he urged historians to avoid—yet the focus of his treatment gives important keys to his view of the age. His emphasis throughout is upon leaders and their actions. Voltaire is full of praise for the skill and successes of the French generals and diplomats, and always insists that Louis XIV was the guiding spirit and prime mover. As for the king's policies that led to chronic warfare, Voltaire occasionally offers limited criticism, such as his comments on the shallowness of the excuses for the Dutch War, but his major emphasis is upon the courage, gallantry, and generosity of the French generals and the glory that they brought Louis XIV. The final and greatest wars of the reign, those of the League of Augsburg and the Spanish Succession, Voltaire treats more as civil wars than wars between nations because of the dynastic issues involved. His patriotism and admiration of this great reign largely neutralized his strong pacifistic sentiment, which is so pronounced in his other works, and caused him to give only the briefest mention of the bloodshed and devastation that resulted from Louis XIV's continual warfare. Significantly, this elitist approach to the period is maintained throughout the work.

Important as Louis XIV's wars were to the record of his reign, Voltaire found the achievements of the French within their borders to be much more indicative of their leadership in the ways of civilization. Their accomplishments ranged from improved conditions of life and massive state-building to the highest intellectual pursuits. These Voltaire describes in great detail, always placing Louis XIV in a position of leadership and causing much to stem from his initiative. Voltaire initially approaches internal affairs through an extensive treatment of "incidents and anecdotes," almost entirely at the royal court. Although these matters may seem trivial in the extreme, Voltaire considered them essential indications of the manners and spirit of the portion of French society with which he was most concerned. There is much on festivals, costumes, and intrigues as well as the glory, pleasures, grandeur, and gallantry that characterized the first part of Louis XIV's personal reign. Always the monarch is shown as dominating his vast army of courtiers through his sense of dignity, imperious mien, and impeccable protocol. The women in his life come in for special attention, particularly Madame de Maintenon, who is extensively praised for her piety, lack of ambition, and devotion to Louis rather than court politics. The final portion of this section presents an appraisal of Louis XIV's qualities and characteristics, which Voltaire held to be crucial to the fortunes of the nation. As always, he stresses the king's dignity, sense of justice, and greatness of soul, and insists that the many criticisms to which he was subjected because of his harsh treatment of the Huguenots and Jansenists, his arrogance toward other rulers, his readiness to undertake devastating wars, and his severity toward many important persons were thoroughly eclipsed by his great qualities and noble deeds. To illustrate his devotion to duty and his high-mindedness, Voltaire quotes extensively for the first time from the important section of Louis XIV's memoirs in which the king himself outlines his concept of his "profession of king." Voltaire even concludes that the Sun King's enormous pride and the many monuments that were erected to his glory were entirely justified by the record of events.

When discussing Louis XIV's extensive program of state-building, Voltaire grapples with the question whether the king or his ministers were responsible for the many achievements of the reign, and he consistently gives the monarch the preponderant role. Colbert's work is presented in detail and is credited with great advances in French prosperity, elements of which Voltaire finds to have survived even the wars in the latter part of the reign. The city of Paris, he joyously remarks, experienced extensive improvements in conditions of life, especially security, and royal patronage aided in the city's beautification. New codes of law enormously facilitated the judicial process, and the military and naval establishments were vastly improved and expanded. Voltaire suggests that Louis XIV might better have spent more money on Paris than on Versailles and made a grievous error in revoking the Edict of Nantes, but, as always, he insists that these lapses were completely outweighed by the king's many successes. In fact, Voltaire boldly concludes that the enormous differences between conditions in France before and after Louis XIV indicate that he did more for his country than any twenty of his predecessors. Proof of this Voltaire found in the changes in manners and customs that occurred during the reign. Factions at court and popular uprisings dwindled, social intercourse became more refined, and many more luxuries and conveniences were readily available. Again the elitist emphasis. All these beneficent changes, Voltaire held, were ultimately the work of the ruler who was the primary influence in molding the life of the nation.

Voltaire's analysis of science, the arts, and letters goes to the heart of the matter, since his chief purpose was to present the cultural climax that France experienced under Louis XIV's aegis. His treatment of the rise of science, chiefly empirical, is brief and dramatic, and is made to parallel the decline of religious authority and superstition. Interestingly, he downgrades Descartes because of his distrust of empiricism, and notes the contributions of the Academy of Sciences but admits that all the great discoveries were made in other countries. Not so in letters, he exclaims, insisting that in this field the French were supreme. And he has little difficulty in establishing this fact merely by pointing to the perfection of the French language and listing the giants in oratory, the drama, and pure literature. Voltaire's exposition reads like an enthusiastic cataloguing of French literary genius during the century, although his emphasis is upon form, style, polish, and rational qualities rather than values and content. Turning to the arts, he indicates the more significant French architectural monuments with the notable exception of Versailles, points to the several academies that were founded during the reign, and pauses over the painters, Poussin, Lebrun, and their successors. When examining the useful arts and sciences, he again looks abroad, stressing the work of Boyle, Halley, Locke, Newton, Mercator, and Leibniz. Voltaire therefore recognizes that much of the cultural climax in Louis XIV's reign was due to foreigners, but he insists that even the international phases of the movement owed much to the king's leadership and support. As evidence he points to the many academies that were founded during Louis XIV's reign, including the French Academy in Rome, his extensive patronage of painters, sculptors, and men of letters, and the many *gratifications* that he accorded large numbers of writers, artists, and scientists both at home and abroad. The king's encouragement of intellectual and cultural pursuits, Voltaire concludes, went far to explain the fact that all Europe was now more enlightened than ever before.

The final section of the *Siècle* deals with religious developments, doubtless the least congenial to Voltaire but obviously
an important element of French civilization. The affairs of the
French Church he discusses under such heads as clerical finances and abuses, the Gallican liberties, the squabble over the
régale, and the Declaration of 1682, avidly noting the slow but
sure decline of superstition that accompanied these debates
over what he regarded as nonessentials. Calvinism he examines
in detail, stressing its partisan, fanatical, and rebellious spirit as
well as the many phases of its persecution under Louis XIV.
The revocation of the Edict of Nantes he deplores both for
pragmatic reasons and because it revived the spirit of fanati-
cism among both Catholics and Protestants. Jansenism he also
heartily disliked. Although he admits a certain greatness among
its ablest proponents—Nicole, Arnauld, Pascal—he viewed it
as pointless disputation and argues that its decline was inevi-
table because of its irrationalism. And quietism for Voltaire was
sheer madness. In closing, he turns to the religion of the Chi-
nese, contrasting their natural virtue, tolerance, and pacifism
with the proselytizing, fanatical, warring religious factions of
Europe.

Even this brief summary of Voltaire's *Siècle de Louis XIV*
indicates that he was attempting to do several things simultaneously: to analyze the elements of French greatness on various
levels, particularly the intellectual and cultural; to emphasize
the crucially significant role of the monarch; and to advance the
philosophes' campaign against Christianity. The latter was
merely incidental, but the others were central to his thesis concerning the significance of the reign and its place in western
history. Voltaire has frequently been accused of oscillating
between his emphasis upon the achievements of the French
people as a nation and his delineation of the sovereign's role
according to the "great man" theory of history. The dichotomy,
however, is more apparent than real, and in fact Voltaire's effort
to do both has the merit of reflecting historical reality. Seventeenth-century absolutism intimately associated the interests,
greatness, and glory of the ruler with those of the nation.
Through able and inspired leadership, the monarch was believed to guide the nation in its many endeavors, cause it to

flourish, and symbolize its greatness. It was in this sense that Voltaire could assert: "He [Louis XIV] never differentiated between his own glory and the welfare of France.... Every king who loves glory loves the public good." The achievements of the French people therefore augmented the prestige of the king, who, in turn, made possible and facilitated their accomplishments through enlightened rule. In this sense the reign was truly the "age of Louis XIV." Although Voltaire's treatment of the period now seems shallow because of his neglect of the great majority of the population and his ignorance of many "deeper" elements of human motivation and historical causation, in its own time his interpretation of the Sun King's reign represented a giant step forward in historical scholarship.

PIERRE-EDOUARD LEMONTEY

Between the publication of Voltaire's *Siècle* and the French Revolution, no perceptible progress was made in interpreting the reign of Louis XIV. And the arrival of the Revolution caused French historical investigation of the seventeenth century to sink to a new low because of the revolutionaries' massive rejection of all that absolute monarchy stood for and their intolerance of all views that were unacceptable to the successive regimes. Under these conditions the few writers who mentioned Louis XIV did little but reflect current prejudices. The best example of a work on Louis XIV by a convinced revolutionary is Jean de La Vallée's *Tableau philosophique du règne de Louis XIV, ou Louis XIV jugé par un français libre,* which was published in Strasbourg in 1791. La Vallée was thoroughly imbued with the doctrinaire liberalism of the Revolution, although he was not blind to certain accomplishments of the old monarchy. In his estimate of Louis XIV, he praised the king's application to the tasks of government, his control of the nobles, his legal reforms, and some of his establishments, such as the Invalides for retired veterans. But he condemned Louis XIV's enormous pride and self-righteousness, his wars, his arbitrary imprisonments by *lettres de cachet,* and especially his personal

tyranny over all others. The greatest evil of Louis XIV's despotism, La Vallée held, was his destruction of human dignity and
the value of the individual. This La Vallée found more damag-
ing to the nation than the king's wars. For this reason he
concluded that the greatest significance of the reign lay in
the growing reaction against the monarch and all that he represented, since this opened the way to the stirrings of liberty
which triumphed a century later in the Revolution.

During the Napoleonic era, Philippe A. Grouvelle added to
the available materials on Louis XIV by publishing his so-called
Œuvres de Louis XIV. Possibly because the Empire brought
renewed interest in the most powerful autocrat in earlier French
history, Grouvelle issued this massive collection consisting
chiefly of Louis XIV's memoirs, many of his letters, and mis-
cellaneous brief tracts. Grouvelle's only original contribution
was his *Considérations nouvelles sur Louis XIV*, which forms
part of the first volume. In his analysis Grouvelle focuses entirely upon the king, his ministers, and his policies. He repeats
the widely accepted contrast between Colbert, the man of
peace and positive contribution, and Louvois, the proponent of
war and military glory, although insisting that the king always
remained the master. Louis XIV's internal policy Grouvelle
found to be his area of greatest achievement because of his success in establishing complete personal domination throughout
his realm. He reduced Montesquieu's much vaunted intermedi-
ary bodies—clergy, nobles, and Parlements—to impotence. By
a variety of clever mechanisms he thoroughly controlled his vast
court and through it the nation. His art therefore lay not in
formulating policy but in ruling men through acts of will. All
this enabled him to make good his idea that his subjects' lives
and goods were his to dispose of as he saw fit. He consequently
abolished the distinction between public and private rights and
created a true personal despotism, the most effective in the history of the French monarchy. Grouvelle significantly refrained
from both praise and blame in describing Louis XIV's despotism, and limited himself to analyzing its elements and effectiveness. His final estimate of Louis XIV was that he lacked
superior intelligence and military talent, and was therefore
neither a great man nor a true hero. But he was a great king.

Although the turbulent years of the late eighteenth and early nineteenth centuries were anything but congenial to objective historical study, one French historian of Louis XIV succeeded in combining scholarly detachment and painstaking research so as to produce important new insights into the reign of the Sun King. He was Pierre-Edouard Lemontey, whose *Essai sur l'établissement monarchique de Louis XIV* was published in 1818. Largely forgotten today, Lemontey was well known in his own time as an expert historian and publicist. He held minor governmental appointments during the Revolution, the Napoleonic Empire, and the Restoration, although his independent means enabled him to go into exile during the Terror. Despite his support of various regimes, he always maintained a large measure of objectivity in his political views. Under Napoleon he was commissioned to write a history of France during the eighteenth century, with the invaluable result that official archives were made available to him. He wrote his *Essai* as an introduction to the longer work, but we now know that his analysis of Louis XIV's reign was his most successful historical study. In it he developed interpretations which added important new dimensions to understanding of the Sun King's place in history and even influenced such outstanding later historians as Ernest Lavisse, Georges Pagès, and Roland Mousnier.

Lemontey was one of those rare historians who combine expert command of their materials with penetrating insights and an ability to express them in striking, meaningful form. His *Essai* is filled with judgments which, although often exaggerated, are invariably food for thought. Throughout his work his constant theme is the unique position of Louis XIV in French history and his crucial significance in the evolution of the nation. Louis XIV, Lemontey claimed, abandoned the traditional foundations of monarchy and created a new system of government which was so powerful that it reordered major elements of the life of the realm and, in fact, sealed the doom of the monarchy itself. In this sense Louis XIV was a true revolutionary, said Lemontey, fully cognizant of the import of his statement. The primary attribute of the new regime, according to his analysis, was its vast power. This Louis achieved by enormously expanding the military establishment, emphasizing the trappings, glory, and other accompaniments of war, and above all by creating a vast, new bureaucracy. Lemontey argued that the latter was Louis XIV's most important personal creation, the true product of his genius and his greatest contribution. More fitting than all the other honors that were bestowed upon him, Lemontey said, would have been the encomium "Louis the Administrator."

For this reason Lemontey maintained that Louis XIV was one of the primary creators of the modern administrative state which eventually made monarchy superfluous. In his own time, however, Louis utilized the great resources of the new system to establish a true personal despotism. This he did by reducing to impotence all elements of the nation that were even remotely capable of challenging his power. The clergy were cowed into submission and maintained themselves only by becoming major supports of the monarchy. The nobles lost their traditional independence and were exploited by the crown for its purposes, while the invidious distinction between the court nobility and the impoverished provincial gentry further weakened the second estate. The Parlement of Paris, the only surviving ancient institution of consequence, was reduced to silence and debarred from the legislative achievements of the reign. Loss of its support by the monarchy was a vital change in this transitional period. As for the bourgeoisie, it was relentlessly regulated, controlled, and exploited. At the same time, the spirit of the reign was made clear to all by constant emphasis upon things military: permanent mobilization in time of peace, pomp and pageantry through endless parades and celebrations, the striking of medals and the erection of statues, and a series of wars that were initiated by deceitful diplomacy and caused inexcusable devastation of many German cities and provinces. Lemontey admitted that certain of Louis XIV's achievements may have appealed to French national pride, but he insisted that this type of rule contained many fatal flaws which would soon destroy it as a viable system of government.

The twin foundations of the regime, Lemontey said, were fear and admiration. These were sufficient as long as the monarchy was successful, but they rapidly weakened with the onset of reverses after mid-reign. Many of Louis XIV's policies also contributed to the decline. Colbert's efforts to promote industry and Louvois's massive expansion of the military machine juxta-posed contradictory and therefore disruptive elements. The new industrialists resented royal despotism and controls, but Louis XIV pushed on with his destruction of rights and liberties and his substitution of a police state for a rule of law. At Versailles, the enormous size of the court and the great emphasis upon protocol isolated the king and his ministers from the mass of the nation, which increasingly feared the aura of mystery that sur-rounded all authority. Admiration slowly changed to hatred among the despised majority. Many of Louis XIV's personal attributes, so great an asset early in the reign, changed to liabil-ities. His belief in his own God-given knowledge of government caused him to assume that he could do no wrong, with the result that too much praise only strengthened his mistaken resolve. After the onset of his fistula (ca. 1682), the tone of all elements of policy seemed to change for the worse. The latter part of the reign witnessed massive persecution of the Huguenots and Jan-senists, Madame de Maintenon's pernicious intrigues, and fi-nally his attempt to place his bastards in the line of succession to the throne. It was a period of defeats abroad and financial chaos at home, compounded by new taxes and confiscations. Degeneration of morality at the court took the form of license, luxury, dissipation, and exploitation, which were feebly masked by endless formalities. Confidence and respect for authority were replaced by questioning, alienation, and fear. The Duc de Bourgogne might have reversed these trends and reestablished the natural ties between the monarchy and the nation, but this was not to be.

For these reasons Lemontey concluded that the historical significance of Louis XIV's reign lay in its disruptive and ulti-mately revolutionary character, as was proved by the fact that traditional monarchy survived Louis XIV only seventy-four years. The Sun King may have been endowed with a certain greatness of spirit and sense of majesty, Lemontey admitted, but his love of power determined both his achievements and his failures. His greatest contribution to the building of France was his creation of the administrative state, but he abused his re-sultant power so extensively that he alienated his subjects and sapped the foundations of the monarchy itself. By simultaneously raising the sovereign to great heights above the people and relentlessly exploiting them, he created a thoroughly untenable situation in which government departed from its true purpose. And after his death the forms of absolutism continued, only to become thoroughly anachronistic when the people beheld despotism everywhere but the despot nowhere. In this way the old monarchy was doomed.

With Lemontey, therefore, we come full circle from Voltaire's laudatory account of Louis XIV's era. With the exception of their agreement concerning his achievements in statebuilding, the two authors are poles apart in their assessments of the Sun King's place in history and his contributions to the life of the nation. The explanation of their divergence undoubtedly lies in the fact that their careers and personal perspectives were separated by the cataclysm of the French Revolution. Voltaire knew firsthand the France that Louis XIV had created, whereas Lemontey witnessed the destruction of absolute monarchy and found major causes of the upheaval in the ruler's mistaken policies. Their personal experiences undoubtedly colored their analyses of past events and caused them to view major elements of their national tradition with very different eyes. In any case, their respective positions provided the two most widely held interpretations of the Sun King's historical significance as France entered the modern era.

2. The Liberal Synthesis

THE "CENTURY OF HISTORY"

The nineteenth century was in many respects the golden age of historical scholarship, and studies of Louis XIV's reign benefited accordingly. Recent experiences with violent political upheavals, which ranged from libertarian to despotic, enabled French historians to view their past from a variety of perspectives and caused them to seek an understanding of their age by examining its roots in earlier centuries. The many schools of thought that enriched French intellectual life during this very prolific period varied greatly in their principles and objectives, but all agreed that their positions represented the fruit of historical experience. Liberalism and nationalism were the touchstones of the major political movements of the century, and both were viewed as owing much to the achievements of earlier generations. The religious revival of the period necessarily turned men's minds toward France's great Christian heritage, while the rich, many-faceted romantic movement provided new insights into human experience in previous ages. Observers who championed civil rights sought their origins in the study of earlier institutions and political practices, and even the socialists developed historical explanations of the causes that they championed. Above all, there was widespread confidence that a knowledge of history facilitated understanding of both the contemporary world and the human condition. All this was accompanied by the development of a rigorous and sophis-

ticated methodology of historical study which revolutionized
the field and, in the eyes of many, raised it to the status of a
science. The nineteenth century has rightly been called the
"century of history."

It was Germany that provided much of the leadership that
was essential to the development of history as an independent
intellectual discipline. The German universities possessed a type
of organization and a pedagogical tradition that enabled them
not only to develop new techniques of research and documentation but also to become fountainheads of the historicism of
which Leopold von Ranke was one of the most famous practi-
tioners. In France, on the contrary, there was considerably less
coordinated effort for the advancement of historical scholarship. Occasional academies of learned men made notable contributions, but no school of thought dominated the field. Indeed,
the most outstanding French historians of the century achieved
their preeminence essentially through their individual efforts.
Although they might indulge in cooperative enterprises, they
retained maximum intellectual independence. The result was
that their personal predilections, especially their political and
religious views, strongly colored their works and occasionally
led them to make premature generalizations. But the risks of
this highly personalized approach to historical study were more
than counterbalanced by the extensive insights that they developed and their contributions to burgeoning historical knowledge. The ablest, furthermore, scrupulously grounded their
analyses of earlier periods upon extensive study of the sources.
This was facilitated by the publication of vast quantities of the
source materials of French history under governmental spon-
sorship. Capitalizing upon his prestige as Minister of Public
Instruction, François Guizot, in cooperation with a number of
leading French historians, founded the Société de l'Histoire de
France in 1833, and soon its monumental publications began to
appear. In this way it might be said that the history of France
became a national institution.

For all their individualism, the great majority of nineteenth-
century French historians who examined Louis XIV's reign
aided in constructing the liberal interpretation of the period.

Although they viewed the Age of Absolutism from their post-revolutionary perspective and generally approved of the more constructive changes that had occurred since 1789, their personal predilections did not necessarily blind them to the monarchy's contributions to the development of the French nation. Instead they were able to place the Sun King's reign in historical perspective and to add extensively to knowledge of its salient features and significance. A few examples will suffice. François Guizot's political philosophy, while excessively rigid, was representative of nineteenth-century liberalism in that he prized maximum liberty under stable government. He therefore praised Louis XIV's extensive state-building and argued that it had been crucial to the growth of modern France. François Mignet held political opinions that were far to the left of Guizot's, but this did not preclude their cooperation. Mignet's most important contribution to knowledge of Louis XIV's reign was his publication of four volumes of documents concerning the Spanish succession, which he undertook at Guizot's request. Very different from both was Jules Michelet, the greatest representative of the romantic school. His memorable descriptions of Louis XIV's wars and persecution of the Huguenots are among the century's most vivid treatments of these matters. The list of French historians who contributed to creating the liberal synthesis might be greatly extended. It is noteworthy that the anti-liberal writers who were instinctively biased in favor of monarchy usually followed Taine's example and limited their attention to the eighteenth century and the Revolution.

As the nineteenth century progressed, the earlier general histories of Louis XIV's reign by such men as Guizot, Sismondi, Michelet, and von Ranke were increasingly supplemented by a vast literature of special studies in which the works of Clément, Rousset, Chéruel, and Boislisle were outstanding. Finally, shortly before World War I, French scholarship reached the point where a new work of synthesis was in order. This was provided by Ernest Lavisse, whose monumental treatment of Louis XIV's reign may be said to have brought the liberal interpretation to fruition. Lavisse's rich and comprehensive analysis remains one of the ablest general histories of the period ever penned.

EARLY GENERAL TREATMENTS

Like so many liberal historians in the nineteenth century, François Guizot viewed western history as a series of dramatic and fruitful episodes, each of which contributed to the growth of human progress and freedom. This position he developed at length in a famous series of lectures which he gave at the Sorbonne in 1828–29 and published under the title *Histoire générale de la civilisation en Europe*. The work was epochmaking as a comprehensive overview of the course of western history from the ancient world to the French Revolution.

Guizot's treatment of the seventeenth century made clear his preference for developments in England rather than France, since it was in England that the clash between monarchy and free inquiry witnessed the triumph of the latter. His analysis of Louis XIV's reign, on the other hand, emphasized its contributions to the growth of the French nation. Taking the position that monarchy had embodied legitimate sovereignty throughout European history, provided her people with indispensable leadership, and enabled them to overcome successive challenges and crises, Guizot found this to be the secret of Louis XIV's great power and the key to the significance of his reign. France during Louis XIV's minority, he recalled, was torn asunder by civil war and was generally discredited, whereas Louis XIV rebuilt the nation and raised it to first rank in Europe. His major instrumentalities were war, diplomacy, administration, and legislation. While admitting that Louis XIV's wars might be criticized on various grounds, Guizot insisted that they were conducted by a legitimate government for a specific purpose, territorial expansion, and were therefore "rational" rather than capricious because their objective was state-building. The consequent acquisitions Guizot found beneficial to France even in his own day. As for Louis XIV's foreign relations, he first developed a highly skilled diplomatic service, regularized practices between states, organized the balance of power, and made France the focal point of international arbitration. Within the realm he made use of the invaluable talents of Colbert and

Louvois to reorganize various administrative bodies and place governmental functions on a permanent footing. These measures he capped by promulgating elaborate ordinances which were true legal codes and added further to national stability. These achievements in state-building, plus royal support of letters and the arts, meant that the monarchy of Louis XIV was a major force in the growth of western civilization.

It is evident that Guizot's chief interest in Louis XIV's reign lay in the development of institutions and the state, and in these areas he found much to admire. But, like Lemontey, he asked why this powerful mechanism declined so rapidly and collapsed in the eighteenth century. His answer resembled Lemontey's, which in fact was commonly accepted among nineteenth-century liberal historians. Louis XIV's monarchy, for all its great strength, rested solely upon absolute power and lacked any basis in popular support, which alone could have perpetuated the governmental system. Free institutions were essential to continuing stability, but these Louis XIV adamantly rejected. Unable to evolve, the monarchy therefore decayed as the nation advanced. The result was that the French people reassumed leadership and developed the spirit of free inquiry which the British had achieved a century earlier. The monarchy of Louis XIV had made important contributions to the growth of the French state, but its inherent vice, absolute power, caused its downfall and rendered it superfluous to the further advance of civilization.

Two multi-volume histories of France that were widely read at this time were Simonde de Sismondi's *Histoire des français* and Henri Martin's *Histoire de France*. Approximately a generation apart, both authors were decidedly liberal and intensely disliked many elements of the Age of Absolutism. Sismondi's family was of Italian origin, had been expelled from Italy in the sixteenth century for political reasons, settled in France and embraced Calvinism, only to be expelled again after the revocation of the Edict of Nantes, this time seeking refuge in Geneva. His hostility to French absolutism thus had a personal foundation, and he freely incorporated his opinions into his historical narrative. Martin held many municipal offices in France after the fall of the July Monarchy, and was ardently republican and anti-clerical. Both sought to compose histories that would present the broad panorama of French history in sufficient depth to give it substance for the general reader, and both devoted more than two decades to composing their respective narratives. Of necessity, their use of unpublished sources was limited, a fact for which Martin especially was criticized, yet both authors achieved wide acclaim and enjoyed extensive followings in their own time. Today their works are chiefly valuable as compilations of known information and expressions of the liberal view of the French past.

Both Sismondi and Martin believed in the didactic purpose of historical study and did not hesitate to judge earlier men and events according to the canons of nineteenth-century liberalism. In one important respect, Martin's treatment of Louis XIV's reign was broader than Sismondi's, since Martin gave extensive coverage of the intellectual and cultural achievements of France during her classic age—-an element that Sismondi largely neglected—yet the two men were agreed on much. Following precedent, they emphasized the positive achievements in state-building that occurred during the first generation after 1661. Martin in particular extensively lauded Colbert, recounting his great accomplishments in many areas despite the enormous obstacles that the king placed in his way, and calling him the last great minister of the French monarchy, with the possible exception of Turgot. Louvois, on the contrary, is generally denounced in these works because of his influence upon the king for war. Both Sismondi and Martin, in fact, unsparingly condemned Louis XIV's wars on all counts. Beginning with the Dutch War, they said, Louis pursued a disastrous foreign policy that was motivated by personal pride and ambititon rather than national interest. His early military successes merely demonstrated the superiority of French arms rather than the French cause. Sismondi praised the Dutch as more heroic than the French aggressors, and Martin named Jan de Witt one of the century's greatest men, who, unfortunately, relied upon reason in an age when Louis XIV's emotions dictated the course of Europe's affairs. Louis's later wars were increasingly motivated by dynastic rather than national purposes and merely succeeded in bankrupting the nation.

Sismondi and Martin likewise agreed in condemning Louis XIV's religious policy, especially his revocation of the Edict of Nantes and his suppression of the Jansenists. Both authors vividly recount the persecution of the Huguenots and attendant barbarities. These they partially attribute to the pernicious influence of Louvois and Madame de Maintenon, but more fundamentally to Louis XIV's detestation of any spirit of independence among his subjects. Religious persecution and constant war inevitably took their toll, they said, causing massive decline on all fronts in the final generation of the reign. Sismondi interpreted this as fitting retribution which was visited upon a misguided absolute monarch who consistently violated the principles of morality and wise government, and he repeated Lemontey's explanation of the monarchy's rapid collapse after 1715. Somewhat more charitable, Martin argued that Louis XIV's virtues and faults were those of his age and he brought the ideal of monarchy to perfection for all time, but he was nonetheless responsible for the rapid decomposition of the monarchy after his death—a development which emancipated the French people and opened the way for the sovereignty of the nation.

Very different in tone and orientation is the work of the great German historian, Leopold von Ranke, *French History, Principally in the Sixteenth and Seventeenth Centuries.* Von Ranke was a foremost practitioner of scientific historicism, and sought in his histories to present an objective picture of "what really happened." For this purpose he deliberately adopted a cosmopolitan viewpoint and prided himself on his extensive knowledge of the source materials in many European archives. His portrayal of Louis XIV's reign is consequently much less partisan and better documented than most French accounts, yet he too upheld the liberal view of western history and had his predilections concerning the ultimate verities in human affairs.

Von Ranke summarized the Sun King's objectives as statebuilding in the most comprehensive sense, subjecting almost all human activities to official controls, and French domination over Europe. He admitted Louis XIV's considerable success in the first area, and recognized that the first generation of his personal reign represented a truly great era in the development of French civilization. When describing Louis XIV's foreign policy, von Ranke attempted to be objective but evidently disliked the threats and duplicity that characterized French diplomacy, and he found little justification for Louis's wars other than his desire for hegemony over all Europe. Even clearer was von Ranke's hostility to Louis XIV's handling of religious affairs, especially his treatment of the Huguenots. Ultimately, he said, Louis XIV's policies were bound to fail because they were based upon false principles: the interests of the state rather than true justice in internal affairs, and deceit and force in foreign policy for national interests rather than the general liberty of Europe. As always, therefore, restraints had to be imposed upon the aggressor nation before Europe could resume her natural growth. And within France this was inevitably accompanied by internal decline, rising criticism, and a broad movement away from all that the Sun King represented.

JULES MICHELET

One of the most personalized and memorable treatments of Louis XIV to be produced during the nineteenth century is contained in the thirteenth and fourteenth volumes of Jules Michelet's *Histoire de France*. Michelet is chiefly remembered as the greatest representative of the romantic school of French historians, but he stood apart from the predominant currents of French historiography and derived his major inspiration from such non-French writers as Vico and Hegel and the romantics generally. Essentially, he developed his own philosophy of history, which represented a unique blend of elements and yet reflected the major assumptions of current liberal thought. As both historian and philosopher, Michelet sought universal meanings in the particulars of past events, and he firmly believed that the past reveals itself through the historian's thoughts and emotions, which provide him with unique insights into the nature and significance of the human drama. Thus the subjective element in Michelet's writings looms very large and frequently contains his most important messages.

The great sweep of human history Michelet viewed as a

titanic struggle for the justice and right that ultimately find their spiritual foundations in every individual. With Vico he believed that history is the product of human conscience and resource, and this provided the basis for his idealization of the people. If there is any hero in Michelet's histories, it is the people, particularly the downtrodden, laboring, morally upright majority. Their lives, hopes, sufferings, and triumphs were for him the stuff of history and the essence of the eternal struggle for liberty. In particular, he idolized the French people above all others, and repeatedly insisted that they were the leaders in the march of western civilization. For all his liberalism and idealism, Michelet was as nationalist as any other devotee of *la patrie.*

Michelet's approach to historical reality through the particulars of human experience was considerably more comprehensive than that of many of his colleagues. Indeed, he prided himself on introducing into historical study many previously neglected disciplines such as linguistics, geography, psychology, and physiology, and attempted to evaluate their influence upon events through their impact upon individuals and entire nations. As much as any modern social scientist, he believed in the interaction between human beings and the innumerable factors that impinge upon their lives, and he sought to present a correspondingly meaningful interpretation of the historical record. If his handling of geography and psychology now appears naïve, it is because of the undeveloped state of these fields in his time. The significance of his methodology is demonstrated by the fact that even today he finds approval among the most advanced French historians. For Michelet, however, it was outstanding individuals and the values that they represented which gave meaning to the stream of history. Realizing that key personalities, particularly men of great power and/or massive followings, often dramatically influence the course of events, he structured his narrative accordingly and gave rulers due recognition in the historical process, but he also viewed them as symbols of forces and values greater than themselves. It was in this vein that he interpreted the historical significance of the greatest men of the past, including Louis XIV. Unfortunately, his volumes on the Sun King's reign are far from his best work.

Written late in his career, they show the influence of both his waning powers and his growing prejudices. To his love of liberty, the French people, and the *patrie*, he now added a virulent anti-clericalism and anti-authoritarianism, both of which caused him to denigrate the monarchy of Louis XIV. His analysis of the reign, however, was as dramatic as it was significant and achieved a special position in liberal French historiography.

In his search for meaning in history, Michelet subjected Louis XIV and his reign to thorough scrutiny and unsparing critical judgment. Unfortunately, Michelet declared, the invaluable contributions of the Renaissance to the advancement of individualism and liberty were snuffed out in the seventeenth century by the triumph of contrary values: authoritarianism, formalism, intolerance, and the use of terror as a political instrument. These even acquired a religious quality which elevated them to the level of dogma. Human reason was not entirely obliterated and survived chiefly in French classic literature, whose greatness he admits, but the regime of the Sun King represented the negation of liberty and human genius, and could only lead to a dead end.

This ultra-critical view of the reign Michelet presents in a series of vignettes and analyses of persons and episodes, often disconnected but building up to a powerful picture. The king is described as an imperious figure, ever conscious of his glory and characterized by a certain greatness, although animated by the wrong ideals. His absolute power and vast resources enabled him to terrorize Europe at a mere whim, said Michelet, pointing to an apparent difference in policy before and after Louis's operation for fistula (1686). Although Louis was served by able ministers, they were simply his tools, Michelet found, insisting that the ruler made and was responsible for all major policies. There is much on Colbert's massive efforts in state-building, and Michelet evidently admired many of his objectives (often negated by Louis) and a few of his achievements. But Colbert he found fundamentally abhorrent because he created an oppressive, tyrannical system of controls and forced it upon the nation. His use of intendants as irresponsible, arbitrary agents Michelet found intolerable and accused them of setting up a police state.

Michelet found that the same spirit motivated Louis XIV's

wars, which consequently had no justification whatsoever and were as much for the purpose of maintaining control over his subjects as foreign conquest. With his formidable war machine, Louis became irresistible at home and the terror of Europe. The War of Devolution was a mere *fête*. More consequential, the Dutch War had no basis but Louis's hatred of the Dutch because they represented all that he despised: self government, bourgeois commercialism, and intellectual liberty. Michelet greatly admired the Dutch for precisely these reasons, and found the "true" Holland to be that of Jan de Witt, the Republicans, and the people generally rather than the "false" Holland of the authoritarian William of Orange. He praised the heroism of the Dutch patriots and insisted that the only result of the war was to arouse Europe against the French aggressor. Later wars, Michelet added, merely bled the nation white and brought general decline on all fronts.

If Michelet's treatment of Louis XIV has a major focus of interest, it is the revocation of the Edict of Nantes. In fact, he claimed that the entire century, because of its authoritarian spirit and values, led to the revocation and was epitomized by it. Many of his chapters present long, graphic accounts of the persecution of the Huguenots, whose austerity, individualism, and industry he genuinely admired. Especially vivid are his accounts of the *dragonnades* and the suffering of those who pitted personal conviction against misguided royal authority. Inevitably, he deplored the Huguenot exodus, pointing to its deleterious impact upon France both at home and abroad and praising the resistance of the Camisards. To Michelet, the revocation, for which he held Louis XIV entirely responsible, presented the Sun King's reign at its worst and most typical.

It is therefore not surprising that Michelet describes the final generation of Louis XIV's reign in the most somber terms as the nadir of the entire history of France. Decline and degeneration characterized all phases of national existence, he found, because Louis XIV's absolutism had absorbed the life of the nation and eroded the vital forces of its people. The king, Michelet claimed, had crushed France's true self and was in this sense a usurper. His baleful impact upon the nation took the form of massive, irresistible controls, exploitive taxation, ruinous war, and depopulation. These were accompanied by moral decay at court, where intrigue and license were the order of the day. Insidious ultramontanism reared its head in the highest circles. Arts and letters declined, and even the most enlightened men, such as Fénelon, merely advocated aristocratic, reactionary reforms. Versailles was sterile, neither alive nor dead, and the nation was adrift. Michelet concluded that Louis XIV initiated nothing but completed much—in fact, he terminated the historical role of absolute monarchy which the French had tried and found wanting. Only in the eighteenth century, when a new spirit and enlightened values once more reasserted themselves, did France rediscover her genius and resume her march toward her true destiny.

ADVANCES IN FRENCH HISTORICAL SCHOLARSHIP

The second half of the nineteenth century was one of the most fruitful periods of French historical scholarship in modern times. The intense patriotism of the age increased Frenchmen's pride in their national past and greatly reinforced the prevailing confidence in the value of historical study. Large numbers of scholars devoted their talents and energies to investigating the roots of French civilization and the role of France in the rise of Europe to world predominance. The result was a massive outburst of historical publications which included scholarly editions of primary sources and a host of monographs by the ablest historians of the age. Inevitably, they gave major attention to the reign of Louis XIV, which many regarded as the climax of French achievements in the pre-revolutionary era and the moment when centuries of earlier French history attained full fruition. Of these extensive contributions to knowledge of Louis XIV and his reign, only the more important, listed topically, will be indicated here.

Nineteenth-century historians were strongly imbued with the importance of outstanding individuals in both shaping and constituting the essentials of the historical narrative, and it was only natural that they should place great emphasis upon the personalities of the king and those around him. This interest in human beings as the core of the historical record evoked considerable interest in Louis XIV's education, ideals, and relations with others. Father Chérot and Henri Druon traced the main lines of his religious and formal education, respectively, in their works, and both concluded that the young king's instruction was deficient in quality and scope but left lasting impressions that sharply influenced his later policies. Considerably more important in forming his character were his initiation into matters of government under the tutelage of Mazarin and his experiences during the Fronde. His relations with Mazarin are carefully examined in two massive histories of France from 1643 to 1661 by Adolphe Chéruel, the editor of Mazarin's letters. Chéruel's works on this period of French history were by far the best before the appearance of Lavisse and adequately place the young ruler in the general narrative. Louis XIV's position during the Fronde is touched upon in Glasson's work on the Parlement of Paris and the Duc d'Aumale's extensive treatment of the great rebel, Condé. These works detail many of Louis XIV's more important early experiences, which he never forgot and which strongly influenced his later relations with his incredibly swollen entourage.

This fascination with key personalities at the center of affairs had other important results in nineteenth-century scholarship. One was the great interest in the memoirs of important persons at court as historical sources. The latter part of Louis XIV's reign was particularly rich in these eyewitness accounts, and scholars labored extensively to produce much needed critical editions of the more important records of this type. Outstanding are the scholarly editions of the memoirs of the Marquis de Dangeau, the Marquis de Sourches, and, above all, Arthur de Boislisle's monumental edition of the memoirs of the Duc de Saint-Simon. The massive erudition of the latter represents nineteenth-century French scholarship at its best and is still invaluable concerning innumerable aspects of Louis XIV's reign.

Still another result of this person-oriented approach to history was the great interest in the court of the Sun King and his life in this extremely formal and elaborate setting. Illustrative of this are two lengthy works which were intended for a wide read-

ing public: Emile Bourgeois, *Le Grand Siècle*, and James E.
Farmer, *Versailles and the Court under Louis XIV*. Appropri-
ately, both authors gleaned most of their information from the
extensive and rich memoirs of the period, and both exhibit a
genuine fascination with Louis XIV and his fabulous surround-
ings at Versailles. The king's personality and character are analyzed with emphasis on his more outward qualities: his charm,
dignity, poise, self-control, and, above all, his majestic bearing,
which impressed all, even his severest critics. His daily routine,
with its endless ceremonial, is recounted in detail, and it is
shown how his mere presence dominated all others. In addition,
both authors describe with evident delight the costumes, *fêtes*,
and generally brilliant and refined life of the court at Versailles.
In fact, both seem to regard the palace and the memory of its
original occupants as great assets to the national history of
France. This intense interest in personalities was also manifest
in many studies of the ladies in Louis XIV's life. His most famous mistresses, Louise de La Vallière and Madame de Montespan, were accorded full-scale, relatively favorable studies by
Arsène Houssaye, Jules Lair, Jean Lemoine, and the very able
Pierre Clément, and all based their works upon extensive examination of the sources. As for Madame de Maintenon, Théo-
phile Lavallée began, albeit unsatisfactorily, the difficult task
of editing her letters, while Auguste Geffroy and the Duc de
Noailles wrote lengthy biographies in which they stressed her
personal virtues and denied that she exercised important influence upon her royal husband's religious policies, especially his
revocation of the Edict of Nantes. Except for those on Madame
de Maintenon, these works are still the best treatments of the
ladies who were closest to the king.

Fittingly, Louis XIV's personal ideals, particularly his understanding of divine-right absolutism, were subjected to new
scrutiny. His views of himself and his mission, at least during
the first years of his personal reign, were made available in the
Dreyss edition of the *Mémoires de Louis XIV pour l'instruction
du Dauphin*, the first critical edition of this important compilation and the basis of much later interpretation of his motivation.
Of major significance concerning the king's political ideology
and much more was Georges Lacour-Gayet, *L'Education poli-*

tique de Louis XIV. This fundamental work not only traces the
young king's political education but examines the extensive literature that contemporaries wrote on the subject and thoroughly analyzes the divine right of kings as it was understood
during the first generation of the reign. The book remains today
the best single treatment of these important matters.

Louis XIV's achievement in rebuilding and extending the
royal administration, which Lemontey so emphasized, provided the focus of the efforts of two of the Grand Monarch's
ablest historians, Arthur de Boislisle and Pierre Clément. Writing approximately during mid-century, Clément is chiefly re-
for his great achievements in many areas despite the manifold
activities of Colbert, whose letters, instructions and memoirs
he edited. Organizing the great minister's records topically,
Clément prefaced each volume with an analysis of Colbert's
work in the area under consideration. These essays were later
collected and published separately. Clément also incorporated
his vast knowledge of the subject into two key works, *Histoire de
la vie et l'administration de Colbert* and *Le Gouvernement de
Louis XIV, ou la cour, l'administration, les finances et le commerce de 1683 à 1689*. In the first he extensively praises Colbert
for his great achievements in many areas despite the manifold
handicaps that the king placed in his path, and in the second
he traces the gradual disintegration of Colbert's system after his
death because of divided authority at the top and such mistaken
policies as the revocation of the Edict of Nantes (which is given
major attention) and continued royal extravagance. Clément
also published a solid study, *La Police sous Louis XIV*, which
examines the work of the two lieutenants general of police, La
Reynie and d'Argenson, in setting up the first police system in
the capital. These works remain basic to all who would investi-
gate these subjects.

Writing approximately a generation later, Arthur de Boislisle made extensive contributions to knowledge of the administrative system in his edition of Saint-Simon's memoirs, which
examines many elements of the government apparatus, particularly the royal councils, and by publishing two important bodies
of source material: the report on the *généralité* of Paris, which
was prepared for the Duc de Bourgogne and gives very detailed

information on economic, social, and institutional life in the area as of ca. 1700, and the *Correspondance des controleurs généraux des finances avec les intendants des provinces, 1683–1715,* which is also a mine of information on administration and finance. Likewise, Jean de Boislisle published the *Mémoriaux du conseil de 1661,* an invaluable record of actions of the royal council during the first year of Louis XIV's personal reign. All these publications complemented the earlier four volumes of *Correspondance administrative sous le règne de Louis XIV,* which were edited by Georges Depping and provide excellent guides to the functioning of all elements of the royal administration. To round out the picture, Hélion de Luçay analyzed the evolution of the secretaries of state and Charles Godard examined the powers and functions of the intendants. The essentials of the great legal cases of the period were made available when François Ravaisson published the *Archives de la Bastille.* Knowledge of Louis XIV's all-important achievements in statebuilding was advancing by leaps and bounds.

Louis XIV's foreign policy and wars were likewise subjected to extensive scrutiny. Indeed, administrative developments and foreign affairs were often treated as but two facets of the Sun King's single, massive effort to increase his power and renown. As Clément had done for Colbert, so Camille Rousset produced the first authoritative and thoroughly documented study of Louis XIV's great war minister in his *Histoire de Louvois.* Here Rousset presents the traditional picture of Louvois, the hard-driving, efficient organizer of Louis XIV's war machine, enjoying great favor with the king, and invariably urging an aggressive policy by any means, be it war, devastation, legal chicanery through the chambers of reunion, or persecution of the Huguenots. Rousset insists, however, that despite Louvois's personal direction of diplomacy and war on many occasions, the king always remained the master, fully aware of policy and always in control. The strong tendency of French scholars to view Louis XIV's foreign policy in thoroughly nationalistic terms after France's defeat in the Franco-Prussian War is blatantly evident in the works of Arsène Legrelle. Although based upon extensive research in the sources, Legrelle's publications are marked by a strong anti-German bias. His *Louis XIV et Strasbourg* thoroughly justifies the annexation of the city as a great creative act and an important step in the building of modern Europe. And his four-volume study, *La Diplomatie française et la succession d'Espagne,* while presenting much valuable information, ultimately praises Louis XIV for his ability and heroism in conducting the war to a successful conclusion, which, Legrelle claims, ended forever the threat of Hapsburg, Germanic domination of Europe and made possible French greatness in the eighteenth century. He even asserts that Louis XIV was motivated by a higher moral sentiment than any of his enemies, that the war demonstrated the moral superiority of France, and that it was therefore France's finest hour. Equally authoritative but much less biased is Cardinal Baudrillart's *Philippe V et la cour de France,* the first volume of which traces in detail the relations between Louis XIV and his grandson from 1701 to 1715 in the context of diplomacy, war, and palace intrigue. The key international agreements of Louis XIV's entire reign were made available in Henri Vast's *Les Grands Traités du règne de Louis XIV.* Shortly before World War I there appeared two significant French theses by historians who were to achieve major recognition during the inter-war years: Georges Pagès, *Le Grand Electeur et Louis XIV: 1660–1688,* and Louis André, *Michel Le Tellier et l'organisation de l'armée monarchique.* The first expertly traces the diplomatic relations between France and Brandenburg-Prussia, and reveals the methods that Louis XIV used when coping with the maze of interests and parties in Germany. The second extensively analyzes Le Tellier's reorganization of the French military establishment before it was taken over by his more famous son, Louvois, and shows how much of the latter's work was initiated by his father.

Louis XIV's policies relative to religious matters, which caused him so much trouble, were carefully but unsympathetically examined by nineteenth-century historians. Their viewpoints can readily be explained by recalling the intellectual currents that were to the fore in this period of intense liberalism, nationalism, and resurgent ultramontanism. Sainte-Beuve's magisterial *Port-Royal* extensively details Louis XIV's persecution of the Jansenists and deplores it as a great tragedy in the history of France and French Catholicism. The work stands as a

monument of French scholarship of its type. Writing from the
ultramontane standpoint, Charles Gérin unabashedly denounced French Gallicanism and Louis XIV's relations with the
papacy in his *Recherches historiques sur l'assemblée du clergé
de France de 1682* and his *Louis XIV et le Saint-Siège*. More
objective is Eugène Michaud, *Louis XIV et Innocent XI*, which
merely shows the king to have been shortsighted and unduly influenced by mediocre counsellors. As for Louis XIV's persecution of the Huguenots and his revocation of the Edict of Nantes,
which dominated so much nineteenth-century thinking about
the Sun King both in France and abroad, again the verdict was
invariably hostile. Charles Weiss, in his *Histoire des réfugiés
protestants de France depuis la révocation de l'édit de Nantes
jusqu'à nos jours*, traced the flight of the Huguenots in detail,
with emphasis on their hardships, and deplored French policy
on all counts. Adolphe Michel attempted to determine Louvois's
role in this affair in his *Louvois et les protestants*, and concluded
that although he did not initiate the harshest measures such as
the *dragonnades*, he supported all acts of violence, more for
political than religious reasons. Frank Puaux contributed much
information on the Huguenots and related matters in a series of
short studies. And the American historian, Henry M. Baird, then
a professor at New York University, exhibited full sympathy
with the persecuted in his voluminous work, *The Huguenots
and the Revocation of the Edict of Nantes*. Indeed, he presents
their history as a tragic epic. Although he insists that Louvois
and Madame de Maintenon were major influences in causing
the persecution and revocation, he maintains that Louis XIV
was thoroughly informed and made all policy decisions. His effort to restore religious uniformity Baird viewed as a grandiose
failure because of the crown's inability to exterminate the Huguenots and the subsequent rise of religious toleration in
France. Such was the strength of nineteenth-century liberalism
that few could understand Louis XIV's actions in terms of his
own ideology and the canons of absolutism.

Although earlier scholars had been aware of the decline of
Louis XIV's fortunes and the growing criticism of his policies
during the last generation of his reign, late nineteenth-century
historians were made increasingly cognizant of this important

countercurrent by a series of publications which set forth in great detail the views of the Sun King's most important critics. To Boislisle's massive edition of Saint-Simon's memoirs was now added Faugère's invaluable publication of the duke's other writings in his *Écrits inédits de Saint-Simon*. A disgruntled but astute observer, Saint-Simon vividly expressed sentiments that were widespread at the royal court. Similarly, a large number of Vauban's writings on many subjects were made available in Rochas d'Aiglun's edition of *Vauban, sa famille et ses écrits, ses oisivetés et sa correspondance*. The key writings of Vauban and Boisguillebert on economic matters were reissued in the convenient Daire edition, and the latter's historical significance was extensively analyzed in Félix Cadet, *Pierre de Boisguillebert, précurseur des économistes, 1646-1714: Sa Vie, ses travaux, son influence*. The political ideas of Archbishop Fénelon, one of Louis XIV's severest critics, were given special attention by many writers, including Paul Janet, Georges Treca, and Jules Lemaitre. Critical editions of important memoirs, such as those of Dangeau and Sourches, also made clear the extent of the criticism of royal policies. All this material provided historians with a deeper understanding of the doubts that were multiplying in the highest circles concerning Louis XIV's omniscience and much that he stood for.

All these publications and hundreds of others mightily expanded knowledge of Louis XIV and the many elements of his reign, the longest in French history. It is noteworthy, however, that the two generations before World War I were remarkably deficient in works of synthesis and interpretation concerning the Sun King's broader significance and his place in history generally. One explanation is that historians were so imbued with the canons of historicism that they limited their efforts to establishing "what really happened" and believed that the facts would speak for themselves. This approach to historical study is evident in the most important cooperative work to appear in France during the late nineteenth century, the *Histoire générale, du IV° siècle à nos jours*, edited by Lavisse and Rambaud. Portions of the sixth volume cover Louis XIV's reign, whose elements are analyzed in individual chapters by outstanding authorities, three of whom—Vast, Lacour-Gayet, and Puaux—

we have had occasion to mention. These authors, particularly Lacour-Gayet, indulge in evaluation of their findings, but the format of the work precluded anything broader. Slightly later, in one of his famous lectures, Lord Acton ventured the generalization that "Louis XIV was by far the ablest man who was born in modern times on the steps of a throne,"[1] and implemented it with a very laudatory account of the reign. Acton took this position because he believed that strong leadership from above was the primary requisite of human advancement in the seventeenth century and that Louis XIV, the greatest of absolute monarchs, fulfilled this role superbly. Acton, however, never went beyond his lectures in developing this theme. And when he planned the *Cambridge Modern History,* the contributors heeded his exhortations to objectivity and impartiality so thoroughly that any evaluations of Louis XIV's reign were quite lacking. In 1911 Jacques Boulenger published his volume *Le Grand Siècle,* but it is merely a bland summary of known information. Clearly the field was open for an outstanding historian who would synthesize the vast accumulated knowledge of Louis XIV and present it according to his own perspective.

ERNEST LAVISSE

This important role fell to the very capable Ernest Lavisse. Building upon the contributions of earlier generations of historians, Lavisse produced a memorable picture of the Sun King and his place in history which at once became authoritative and still commands considerable respect. In fact, much of the information that he assembled is still regarded as fundamental to an understanding of the reign. His analysis of Louis XIV's character, policies, and momentous impact upon the historical development of France is brilliant and in part idealized, yet he did not hesitate to indulge in criticisms of this greatest of French monarchs, whom he both admired and censured for his incessant efforts to fulfill his ideology of grandeur.

Lavisse was thoroughly imbued with the ideals of his time,

1. *Lectures on Modern History* (London, 1956), p. 234.

liberalism and patriotism, and these exercised unmistakable influence on his view of earlier French history. In particular, his patriotism was of the most virile sort, as is evidenced in his textbooks. If the hero of Michelet's history is the French people, that of Lavisse is the French nation. As editor and contributor to the collaborative, multi-volume *Histoire de France*, however, he attempted to be more historicist, but the stamp of his personal ideals is evident throughout. Of the three volumes, all dated 1911, that are devoted to Louis XIV's reign, Lavisse himself wrote the first two, which carry the narrative through 1685, and the conclusion of the third, which treats the period of decline, 1685–1715. The others who contributed to the third volume—Saint-Léger, Saguac, and Rébelliau—present copious information on all aspects of the last generation of the reign, but their stated views of its significance thoroughly accord with those of Lavisse. Whether this resulted from a genuine consensus or from Lavisse's influence as editor is impossible to determine, but their identity of views is striking. Be that as it may, Lavisse's *Histoire de France* has consistently been rated as one of the most successful collaborative works in historical scholarship.

Like many of his predecessors, Lavisse evinced considerable interest in Louis XIV's personal characteristics and ideals. After describing his charm, reserve, prudence, sense of justice, and devotion to the obligations of kingship, Lavisse focuses upon what he considers to be the king's most important characteristic —his boundless egotism. In fact, Lavisse goes so far as to make this both the keynote of Louis XIV's reign and the explanation of his most momentous policies. Louis XIV's supreme egotism, which caused him to place himself over all and to view all in terms of himself, troubled Lavisse, who felt that it was not truly French and attributed its inspiration to the king's Spanish mother. Likewise, the extreme formalism of his court, his readiness to fuse political and religious matters, and his reliance upon swollen bureaucracies Lavisse ascribed to imported Spanish influences. These, he added, were massively reinforced by the prevailing idea of divine right of kings, which Louis XIV carried to its furthest limit. From infancy he was taught that he was "God-given," divinely destined to absolute rule over the greatest nation of Europe. He believed that he was the image of God on earth, that all should accept on principle this religion of monarchy, and that all should willingly submit to his dictates. Hence his perennial concern for his personal glory, which seemed literally destined by divine decree. The result was that he measured all in terms of himself, his interests, prestige, and glory, which he equated with those of the nation.

With such a view of Louis XIV's reign, it is not surprising that Lavisse was both fascinated and repelled by many of its signal features. This is markedly apparent in his treatment of Louis XIV's immensely swollen court after the building of Versailles. Here Lavisse presents glowing descriptions of the buildings, decorations, gardens, fountains, and, above all, the festivals that dazzled the king's contemporaries. But Versailles he viewed as much more than the most lavish abode of the Sun King. A vital instrument of government, that is, control, Versailles housed great numbers of nobles and bureaucrats who functioned as an enormous clientele and whose sole purpose was to grace the king's presence and carry out his bidding. The entire life of this vast establishment revolved around the king, and all others were "small" in his presence. The symbolism of Versailles, deliberately contrived to impress contemporaries, presented Louis XIV as a god enthroned in a universe of his own making, one in which all was regulated through ever-present ceremonial and in harmony with its creator. And Lavisse leaves no doubt that Versailles effectively increased the king's glory and renown throughout Europe. The other side of the coin, which Lavisse equally emphasizes, was Versailles's great cost in lives and money and its adverse effects upon Colbert's efforts to reform the royal finances. Lavisse also stresses the increasing falsity and corruption of the court during the latter part of the reign, when the gaiety of the earlier years died away and Versailles merely masked the decline of much that the Sun King stood for.

Turning to royal policy, Lavisse at once underscores one of his most significant interpretations of Louis XIV's reign, namely, the king's rejection of Colbert's offer to rebuild the French economy as the basis of a newly powerful France. By reading Clément's edition of Colbert's letters and his several studies of the

great finance minister's work, Lavisse concluded that Colbert
came forward early in Louis XIV's personal reign and proposed
to render France rich and powerful and her monarch glorious
by massive application of the economic principles that were
later known as mercantilism. Specifically, the objective was to
increase the monetary wealth of the realm by expanding pro-
duction of necessities and luxuries and multiplying exports so
as to achieve a favorable balance of trade. To do so required
great effort to overcome the disorganization and inefficiency of
French industry through massive regulation, reforming the system of taxation, developing an empire, and building a navy and
merchant marine. For this purpose the realm should be disci-
plined and organized for maximum gain, while its life would be
directed by a prudent, economical ruler who would be as famil-
iar with his merchants as his soldiers. Lavisse recognized that
this proposal necessitated revolutionary departures from the
traditional social and political ideology that the French kings
and the elite of the nation had followed for centuries, yet he
repeatedly deplores Louis XIV's rejection of Colbert's offer as a
great error of policy and one that was fraught with dire consequences for the French monarchy in the following century.
Because Louis XIV never adjusted to the change in values that
Colbert's offer necessitated, Lavisse maintains, he sought renown through the traditional means that were embedded in the
monarchical ideal: increased control at home and aggrandize-
ment abroad. Fundamentally, Louis viewed Colbert merely as
a valuable functionary whose duty it was to provide funds for
purposes that were higher than mere monetary gain. The result
was that Colbert labored against insuperable obstacles during
his entire ministry. Although he accomplished much in many
spheres, he was ultimately defeated by the king's different prior-
ities.

Lavisse extensively demonstrates the effectiveness of Louis
XIV's controls over French society by examining its evolution
from this standpoint. In fact, this is his sole approach to the
changes within French society in this period, reflecting his conviction that royal policy was by far the most influential factor in
channeling the growth of the French nation. He examines the
impact of royal policies upon the lower classes, officeholders,

nobility, and clergy, showing how conditions of life were altered for each, generally worsening the lot of the great majority
while reserving certain favors for the elite. He also indicates the
extent of the king's successes in increasing controls over such
quasi-autonomous bodies as the courts, guilds, municipalities,
and provincial estates. The major organs of opinion, chiefly the
press, were also sharply regulated, and even the arts and many
branches of learning were regimented through the academy
system, all according to the canons of classicism for the purpose
of royal glorification. Lavisse concludes that Louis XIV's reduction of his subjects to obedience in this fashion was one of his
clearest successes.

The same could not be said for Louis XIV's policies concerning religious matters, and Lavisse generally deplores the king's
handling of all major religious issues during his reign. His relations with the Jansenists were marred by mistakes, compromises, and unjustified persecution which left bitter resentment.
His support of Gallicanism seemed successful at first but was
later undermined by extensive concessions. As for Louis XIV's
efforts to extirpate Protestantism, Lavisse presents the narrative
in great detail with evident sympathy for the persecuted. Indeed, the revocation of the Edict of Nantes and its aftermath
are recounted as massive fiascoes, reprehensible on all counts.
Louvois and Madame de Maintenon are allowed a certain limited influence upon events, and Lavisse argues that the king
was not always informed of the worst excesses, but he insists
that Louis was always in charge of policy and determined its
thrust at any given moment. These many errors in Louis XIV's
religious policies Lavisse accounts for by recalling the king's
belief in the sacerdotal character of royalty, and to this extent
he attempts to explain Louis's miscalculations in contemporary
terms. But Lavisse also indulges in hindsight when he decries
the king's policies as disastrous because of the opposition that
they engendered—opposition which grew in subsequent generations and undermined the monarchy itself.

As all historians know, Louis XIV's foreign policy and wars
were major elements of his reign and his striving for personal
glory, and Lavisse gives them corresponding emphasis. It is in

this area that his French patriotism is most evident, writing as he did during the aftermath of the Franco-Prussian War, which he had witnessed as a young man. The traditional objective of French foreign policy he believed to have been the attainment of France's natural boundaries, those of ancient Gaul. Sully and Richelieu had sought this by allying France with the lesser powers of Europe against the dominant Hapsburgs and moving defensively, with great caution. Lavisse held that Louis XIV followed this tradition but with a major difference. Abandoning the prudence of earlier kings and ministers, he now indulged in open aggression, gradually losing his allies and risking confrontation with all Europe. Lavisse believed that Lous XIV realized the evident dangers of such a policy but was pushed to this extreme by his ideology of grandeur and his determination to achieve hegemony over all Europe, come what might. Lavisse admired the king's war machine, that is, Louvois's army and Colbert's navy, calling them the most successful products of the many administrative reforms, but he deplored Louis's diplomacy, which was characterized by threats, ruses, and acts of violence short of war.

From his nationalistic perspective, Lavisse ascribes a certain significance to each of the Sun King's wars. The War of Devolution he deplores not because of any injustice but because of Louis's failure to annex the Spanish Low Countries and to incorporate them into the French nation. This he repeatedly criticizes as one of the greatest mistakes of the reign, a historic lost opportunity for France. And the Dutch War he finds significant because it presented an unparalleled occasion for occupying the left bank of the Rhine. Again it was Louis's indecision that compromised later French national growth. As for Louis XIV's later wars against almost all Europe, Lavisse finds them punctuated by heroism and expertise on the part of the French but hardly worth the price. Although he occasionally lauds French victories and finds a certain greatness of spirit in the aged king when faced with defeat, Lavisse nevertheless condemns Louis XIV's foreign policy as a failure during both generations of the reign—the first because of his unwillingness to pursue his objectives when circumstances were uniquely favorable, and the second because his egocentric policies exacted enormous sacrifices that were not justified by commensurate gains.

Throughout this analysis of Lavisse's estimate of Louis XIV, we have consistently presented royal policy as determined by the king rather than his ministers. This is deliberate. When analyzing the respective roles of Louis XIV and his most powerful ministers, such as Colbert and Louvois, Lavisse ascribes them important functions but insists that all major decisions were the king's. "It seems," says Lavisse in a key statement, "that Louis XIV was never directed as much by those around him as is believed. It may be quickly said that he first followed Colbert and then Louvois. The truth might well be that Colbert's manner first was congenial to him and later that of Louvois, and that the favor of the one and then the other corresponded to two phases of Louis XIV's life."[2] And in an important article in the *Revue de Paris,* Lavisse shows how Colbert developed proposals which he urged upon the king by various means and often implemented as he chose, but that the king opposed him on many occasions, rejecting or revising his recommendations and always retaining direction of official policy. This position is crucial to Lavisse's estimate of Louis XIV's place in history. Since he believed that Louis was always in control of the work of his ministers and that his major decisions stemmed from his ideology of kingship, Lavisse felt warranted in ascribing all praise or blame to the ruler alone. And when it is recalled that Lavisse believed royal policy to have been the great dynamic element shaping the evolution of the French nation during Louis XIV's reign, his view of the Sun King's place in history understandably assumes momentous proportions.

This assumption that royal policy was the most decisive factor in national development was characteristic of the period when Lavisse was writing. It obviously ascribes major practical import to human decision and, unlike more recent historical scholarship, tends to discount the limitations that are imposed upon rulers by prevailing conditions. Optimism concerning the efficacy of human action was fundamental to the liberalism of Lavisse's time, and it is not surprising that he made it the corner-

2. *Histoire de France,* vol. 7^2, p. 60.

stone of his estimate of Louis XIV, whom he viewed as the most
powerful and influential king in French history. Although Lavisse was entirely aware of the fact that conditions within the
realm placed great obstacles in the part of efficient government,
he nevertheless felt justified in judging Louis XIV according to
the fruits of his policies and from the standpoint of unrealized
alternatives.

It was this approach to Louis XIV's place in history that determined Lavisse's estimate of the reign. Briefly stated, Lavisse
concluded that Louis XIV marvelously fulfilled his ideal of divine-right absolutism and brought the French monarchy to its
final historical form, but that in so doing he bankrupted the state,
failed to achieve the necessary reforms, aroused extensive hostility both at home and abroad, and ossified the monarchy to
the point where it was incapable of further development. In
other words, Louis XIV's reign represented both the fruition
and the termination of the monarchy's contributions to the
growth of the French nation and exhausted the potentialities of
monarchy itself. Furthermore, these contributions might have
been greater if Louis XIV had pursued different policies in advancing the French cause. Among his many errors Lavisse especially deplored his rejection of Colbert's offer to place the
French state on a sound economic basis, his failure to make
France a great sea power, and his neglect of the opportunity to
annex the Spanish Netherlands. Lavisse recognized that the first
resulted from Louis's thoroughly traditional values relative to
the most prestigious concerns of kings, that the second reflected
the equally traditional French orientation toward land warfare,
and that the third stemmed from the king's reluctance to undertake all-out war early in his personal reign, but these historical explanations did not deter Lavisse from criticizing Louis
XIV for failing to pursue French interests in ways that would
have contributed to future national growth. For all the vogue of
historicism, this reading back of later experiences and values for
purposes of historical judgment was widespread in Lavisse's
time and seems unhistorical in the extreme.

Writing from this standpoint, Lavisse regrets the fundamental and unsurprising fact that the Sun King sought glory
only through traditional means. His achievements were many

and his leadership directed French efforts during this period of brilliance in the arts of civilization and French preponderance over Europe. The king's clearest success Lavisse found in his reduction of his subjects to obedience, but the result was that he mistakenly believed it sufficient to be strong. Thus the monarchy lost its indispensable roots in the French people, and its final form was none other than despotism. But despotism was not a viable form of government for France because no subsequent monarch could fill the place of the Sun King. In the next reign the regime rested upon tottering foundations, said Lavisse, quoting Lemontey, for even as the memory of Louis XIV's brilliance was being revived and admired by such as Voltaire, men "found despotism everywhere but the despot nowhere," and the monarchy survived the Sun King only seventy-four years before it succumbed. The reader is left with the impression that Lavisse revered the reign of Louis XIV as a productive, dramatic, and crucially significant moment in history, when France fulfilled her ideal of absolute monarchy under the Sun King's leadership, but that this ideal proved wanting in practice and was perforce discarded when the nation resumed its growth along different lines.

3. Twentieth-Century Revisionism

BETWEEN TWO WORLD WARS

As the twentieth century progressed, historical scholarship concerning the reign of Louis XIV increasingly assumed the form of revisionism. Because the basic outlines of the period had been established by nineteenth-century scholars and synthesized by such authorities as Lavisse, the major remaining task was held to be further investigation of topics whose importance had been demonstrated but were imperfectly known. This additional research invariably took the form of more thorough probing of the relevant sources and the publication of monographs which set forth additional information and revised understanding of specific topics to a greater or lesser degree. In the process much light was shed upon many elements of Louis XIV's reign, but few revolutionary changes in accepted views were made. This was especially true of the works that appeared during the two decades between World Wars I and II. At that time certain new schools of thought were gaining recognition (notably the *Annales* school, to be discussed below), but none significantly altered accepted views of Louis XIV. The result was that historians directed their efforts toward increasing knowledge of the Sun King's reign essentially along traditional lines. Publication of source material sharply declined during the period between the wars and never again equaled the output of the previous century. A limited number of general works on Louis XIV's reign were produced, important chiefly for their reinterpretation of known materials. Most significant were the scholarly monographs that analyzed certain key topics in depth. Of these, only the most outstanding will be mentioned here.

The two most interesting general treatments of Louis XIV to appear in the 1920s were those of Louis Madelin and Georges Pagès. Both were outstanding historians although representative of very different schools of thought. Madelin's portrayal of Louis XIV occupies a hundred pages in his *Histoire politique, de 1515 à 1804,* and Pagès examines the reign in the second half of his brief but important book, *La Monarchie d'ancien régime en France (de Henri IV à Louis XIV).* Neither work is devoted exclusively to Louis XIV, and neither superseded Lavisse, but both are important for their interpretations of the essentials of the reign and its place in the growth of the French nation.

Madelin and Pagès were similar in being very able historians, but they differed markedly in their interests and weighting of essentials. Madelin was the more prolific, producing many lengthy studies of the old regime and the revolutionary and Napoleonic periods. His works are characterized by considerable grace of style and extensive insights that reflect his strong rightist orientation. Pagès was more the professional researcher and scholar. A professor at the Sorbonne, he was more neutral in his personal views and made institutional history his forte. And he was certainly one of the most outstanding French historians of the inter-war period. The sharp differences between his views and Madelin's on Louis XIV graphically demonstrate how very competent scholars can find widely divergent meanings in much known information. In the 1930s David Ogg published his biography of Louis XIV, and Philippe Sagnac and A. de Saint-Léger collaborated on their volume in the Peuples et Civilisations series, *La Préponderance française: Louis XIV (1661–1715).* Both are successful, politically oriented informational presentations, but neither attempts any reinterpretation of the reign.

To return to the views of Madelin and Pagès, the most striking theme in Madelin's overview of Louis XIV's reign is his evident admiration of the king. Louis XIV he presents as attractive, able, and moderate, with much common sense, and, above all, determined to govern effectively, thereby fulfilling his destiny. And for Madelin as well as Louis XIV, this meant the reestablishment of order in all things. "Order!" Madelin exclaims almost in rapture. "It is undeniably through order that the government governs, the administration administers, the courts render justice, commanders limit themselves to war, the artisan works, the merchant trades, and the laborer labors without anything interrupting the regular and methodical work of the whole nation. And it is especially through order that the king reigns, he, too, performing 'his craft.' "[1] This was the ideal of Louis XIV's contemporaries, Madelin found, and in it lay the king's strength. Accordingly, it was for the purpose of reestablishing order that Louis XIV supported Colbert's many reforms, subjugated all classes, municipalities, and provinces, codified the laws, subdued the courts, and even sought unity in religion by suppressing the Jansenists and extirpating Protestantism, all of which were thereby justified. Successes in these areas plus victories in war brought Louis XIV to the pinnacle of his fame and power at mid-reign.

But for all his admiration of Louis XIV, Madelin recognizes that the tone and very qualities of his rule changed in the 1680s. Colbert's peaceful reforms were replaced by Louvois's use of force and Madame de Maintenon—symbols of a hardening of spirit of which the revocation of the Edict of Nantes was a part. And after Louvois's death, undiluted absolutism was the order of the day. Madelin duly chronicles the defeats abroad, financial chaos at home, and the rise of criticism, calling these massive threats to the entire realm. But the aged king he pictures as doing his duty by maintaining his fortitude and appealing to the nation, which responded in kind. Thus Louis XIV, through Marshal Villars and his victory at Denain, once more restored order and preserved the king's sacred trust. For all his recognition of the dismal record of the last generation of the reign, Madelin paints Louis XIV as an admirable, heroic figure who persevered to the end and saved France. This plus his early accomplishments caused Madelin to place Louis XIV among the great

1. *Histoire politique,* p. 304.

builders of France, in the direct line from the medieval kings
to the revolutionaries and Napoleon.

Very different and somewhat more traditional was Pagès's
interpretation of Louis XIV's reign. True, Pagès was less concerned with the king and more with the monarchical system of
government than Madelin, yet he always placed Louis XIV at
the center and found him the arbiter of policy. Pagès dwells
extensively on the first ten years of Louis XIV's personal reign as
the great constructive period. This he interprets as the personal
and common work of Louis XIV and Colbert, describing the
latter as the king's chief aide and a major force because of his
personal direction of affairs. Pagès therefore weights very heav-
ily Colbert's personal contributions to state-building, and his
accomplishments in many areas are duly noted with evident
approval. While Louis XIV is always designated the architect
of policy, Colbert is shown to have been the prime mover in its
fulfillment. In addition, much attention is given to administrative reforms and the subjugation of all elements of French
society. Regarding the latter, however, Pagès echoes Lemontey
by pointing to the increased use of force, that is, the army and
the police, to coerce all classes and the tendency of the regime
to become a military despotism.

More important than these rather traditional views is Pagès's
treatment of the last generation of Louis XIV's reign. This
period he calls the "deformation," the years that witnessed the
ruination of the monarchical system that Louis XIV and Colbert
had so carefully constructed. And Pagès makes it clear that he
believed Louis XIV's policies to have been the major cause of
this disaster. It began with Louvois, whom Pagès presents as a
sinister influence, pushing Louis XIV toward war and having
even greater influence than Colbert. In fact, he speaks of a brief
"reign of Louvois." Unfortunately, Louvois's disappearance in
1691 did not end Louis XIV's propensity for war, the chief cause
of the debacle. To these adverse factors were added the king's
unchecked personal absolutism and massive expansion of the
bureaucracy. The intendants in particular introduced arbitrary
procedures that aggrieved all elements of the population. The
nobles were reduced to subservience with war as their only
occupation, and the crown completely failed to develop a new

place for them in French society—a national tragedy. Royal policies relative to the Jansenists, Huguenots, and even the Gallicans gave rise to extensive opposition and turmoil, while constant exploitation of the nation's human and material resources caused vast misery—all because of mistaken royal policies. These inevitably gave rise to widespread criticism, which is presented in detail. In this way Pagès indicates that the monarchy of Louis XIV had clearly veered off course and was rapidly losing the support of all elements of the nation.

Pagès's conclusion concerning the place of Louis XIV's reign in French history is a classic statement of this viewpoint. After listing the many contributions of the monarchy to French national growth through the seventeenth century before its "deformation," Pagès adds:

> But although it had accomplished a national work, it was unable to give its authority a national foundation. It remained a prisoner of the past. It retained the ancient characteristics of personal monarchy and was unable to develop without emptying of substance those institutions that might have served to sustain it. It committed the irreparable error of believing that it sufficed for a government to be strong. At the end of the seventeenth century—to borrow from Lavisse the figure that he himself borrowed from Lemontey—"the columns with which royalty was supported were hollow." The administrative reforms created by Louis XIV and Colbert provided no remedy: they merely increased the strength of the governing power but did not associate it with the nation. In the presence of society that was changing, the monarchy of the old regime had become incapable of parallel change. It was doomed.[2]

It hardly need be added that Pagès and Madelin differed drastically concerning Louis XIV's place in the development of the French nation.

These books of Madelin and Pagès are not entirely representative of twentieth-century revisionism, which usually signifies rectification of historical knowledge through intensive research in limited areas. The period between the wars, however, produced many scholarly monographs of this type, and they frequently increased understanding of Louis XIV. One of the ablest and most successful was Marc Bloch's massive study

2. *La Monarchie d'ancien régime*, pp. 214–15.

Les Rois thaumaturges. A thorough work of a very high order,
the book represents intellectual history at its best and may be
regarded as the definitive treatment of its subject. Its theme is
the sacred character of royalty in the medieval and early modern
periods, as this was demonstrated by the kings' use of the royal
touch to cure scrofula. Although the book examines this practice in England and France from the early Middle Ages to its
decline in the eighteenth century, it analyzes important elements of the religion of monarchy that were generally accepted
in Louis XIV's time and which he thoroughly believed. The
coronation of the king at Rheims climaxed with the ceremony
of consecration in which he was anointed with holy oil. Through
this sacramental unction he was believed to be reborn into a
mystical life, literally a changed being with unusual powers.
Hence the sacerdotal character of royalty and the generally
accepted religion of monarchy. Its most graphic evidence was
the ceremony of the royal touch which Louis XIV regularly
held on feast days at designated times and places. Great crowds
invariably appeared seeking the miraculous cure, and Louis
XIV obliged by performing the ceremony throughout his entire
reign, touching 1,700 persons on the last occasion less than three
months before his death. Only toward the end did slight traces
of skepticism appear in the most advanced intellectual circles,
but the great majority in all levels of society continued to be-
lieve. The study thoroughly investigates this vital element of the
ideology of monarchy and thereby throws considerable light on
Louis XIV's understanding of kingship and his motivation in
determining policy.

Considerably less valuable were two publications that
touched upon Louis XIV's personal life. In 1923 Jean Longnon
issued a simplified, uncritical edition of Louis XIV's memoirs,
which added a few elements to those in the earlier Dreyss edition and is considerably easier to use but otherwise marked no
advance. Meeting criticism, Longnon published a slightly en-
larged but still uncritical version in 1927. While these volumes
made certain texts readily available, they did nothing to clear
up the controversy concerning the nature and value of the
memoirs, which were written chiefly by Périgny and Pellisson
rather than the king. Madame de Maintenon, the last lady in

Louis XIV's life, was the subject of two important publications by Marcel Langlois: an article in the *Revue historique* and a brief biography. These closely reasoned studies are based upon a careful analysis of her correspondence, much of which he later edited. Unlike her earlier biographers, Langlois paints Madame de Maintenon as a very unsympathetic figure: grasping, arrogant, intolerant, and constantly domineering over others. As for her possible influence upon Louis XIV's policies, particularly those concerning religious matters, Langlois shows that she never attended council meetings and had no direct, demonstrable influence on the course of events. On the other hand, her royal husband told her all and she intensely desired to wield influence in many areas. The result was that she used oblique methods to this end, with subtle but indeterminate effect. Langlois's studies contribute certain insights into the realities of the latter part of Louis XIV's reign, but much remains to be done in this area.

Regarding Louis XIV's relations with Colbert, whose "offer" to the king of an economically sound France so dominated Lavisse's treatment of the reign, knowledge was expanding during the inter-war period but essentially along traditional lines. In 1926, Henri Sée reviewed in the *Revue historique* the gains of the intervening years and concluded that with the exception of his overstressing the breadth and "revolutionary" nature of Colbert's ideology, Lavisse's treatment remained sound. Six years later Prosper Boissonnade published the fruit of thirty-six years of research in a massive study devoted to Colbert's work in strengthening French industry. Boissonnade molded his entire volume about the theme of *"étatisme,"* that is, state control over all aspects of industrial activity. Colbert he regarded as the great historic exemplar of this economic statism in action, and he shows with a mountain of evidence how he applied his comprehensive program of regulation, subsidization, and protection to major segments of French industry. As for Louis XIV, Boissonnade pictures him as docilely following Colbert's initiatives, not only giving them royal approval but lending them his prestige by frequent visits to the major royal factories. The credit for Colbert's successes in this area should therefore go to him and only incidentally to the king. Boissonnade argues that statism of this type was a natural component of absolutism, that Colbert was its master practitioner, and that his contributions to French industrial growth long outlived him.

In 1939, Charles W. Cole published his two thick volumes on Colbert, which analyze the economic aspects of the great finance minister's work in a broader, more traditional, and less perceptive way than Boissonnade. Cole, like Boissonnade, based his work on extensive investigation of the sources and surveys Colbert's many-sided activity in detail. Regarding Colbert's relations with the king, Cole merely presents the usual picture of a hard-working minister receiving continual but precarious support from his sovereign, who placed great obstacles in his path. Today the work is valuable as a compilation of much specific information but no more. Clearly, the work of historians in this area was proceeding along strictly traditional lines. This was further demonstrated in the same year when Henri Sée issued his *Histoire économique de la France: Le Moyen Âge et l'ancien régime.* Patently a work of synthesis, Sée's book incorporates the findings of Boissonnade and a great many others and presents copious information but with only slight variations from the views that were adumbrated by Lavisse. For all his effort to place the economic policies of Louis XIV and Colbert in their broader context, Sée continued the tradition of moving outward from the center rather than the reverse—an orientation that was coming increasingly into question in other quarters.

One specialized work added considerably to knowledge of Colbert's work in rebuilding the French navy. This was the fifth volume of Charles de La Roncière's *Histoire de la marine française.* Here Colbert's monumental efforts are presented in detail and the extent of his success is carefully measured. Louis XIV's well-known lack of interest in the navy, as compared with his love of his army, is somewhat modified in La Roncière's account. He shows Colbert resorting to various tactics, such as installing a miniature fleet and staging mock battles on the Grand Canal at Versailles, for the purpose of arousing the king's interest, but these maneuvers were only partially successful. More important to Louis XIV, La Roncière argues, was the significance of the navy—or lack of it—relative to his *gloire.* He consequently followed the successes and failures of his navy with keen interest, and he was adamant that the fleets of all other nations, including the powerful English and Dutch, salute the French by dipping the flag on all occasions, in both the Atlantic and the Mediterranean. But Colbert never succeeded in gaining Louis XIV's full support for his navy—a fact that added greatly to his disillusionment during his last years.

Louis XIV's relations with his other great minister, Louvois, were explored in a work of primary importance, Louis André's *Michel Le Tellier et Louvois*. Continuing his investigation of this famous father-and-son team, André produced a study that was much superior to the earlier Roussel in both its precision and its documentation. The work is almost a dual biography in that it traces the careers and accomplishments of both men to 1685, the date of Le Tellier's death, and stresses their close cooperation during more than two decades of royal service. Their manner and methods were different—Le Tellier habitually moved with steady, unspectacular, limited measures, whereas Louvois was more forceful and imperious though equally efficient—but they were alike in devoting all their energies to serving their king. Regarding Louis XIV's precise relations with Louvois, André shows that the latter was not only a great administrator but assumed a major role in the diplomacy of the period. Indeed, André pictures Louis XIV and Louvois as planning both diplomatic and military strategy in concert, deliberately coordinating them for maximum effect—a vital relationship which often determined the course of events. The king always had the last word, but Louvois was all-important in the execution of official decisions, which, in fact, he had influenced in their formative stages. As for Louvois's role in the persecution of the Huguenots, however, André uses copious documentation to show that throughout the entire episode Louvois was merely the loyal, devoted royal servant and no more. Before the revocation of the Edict of Nantes he conveyed the king's decrees to the provinces and saw to their execution, largely because he regarded the Huguenots as troublemakers and in certain instances actual rebels. Also for this reason he approved of forceful measures, although he did not invent the *dragonnades,* and after several years of experience with them he moderated their worst excesses as contrary to the royal desires.

In other words, Louvois viewed the Huguenot problem from the perspective of a secretary of state for war and a soldier rather than a religious partisan. If he approved of the revocation, in this he merely echoed general sentiment at the court. Throughout, therefore, André insists that all responsibility for the policy of persecution and extirpation of heresy lay with the king.

During the inter-war years, gains in knowledge of Louis XIV's role in the far-reaching institutional and administrative reforms of his reign unfortunately fell far short of the potential of French scholarship. At that time three talented, outstanding authorities were active: Georges Pagès at the Sorbonne, Edmond Esmonin at the University of Grenoble, and François Olivier-Martin at the Law Faculty in Paris. All had great knowledge of this field but published very little. In addition to his work that is analyzed above, Pagès issued many studies of seventeenth-century institutions, but most of these stop short at the beginning of Louis XIV's personal reign in 1661. A valuable exception is a serialized article that he published in the *Revue des cours et conférences* on the French administrative system in the final period of Louis XIV's reign. Here Pagès traces in very general terms the decline of the councils and the rise of officials and administrative bodies to new importance, creating a vast bureaucracy that was directly subject to the king and served as a vital tool of personalized absolutism. And Pagès shows the extensive growth of the intendants' powers which resulted in increasingly despotic controls. All this, however, is presented only as an overview and leaves the reader wanting much more. Otherwise Pagès's views of administrative developments during Louis XIV's personal reign are available only in hard-to-find mimeographed notes for his courses.

The ultra-meticulous Esmonin had an unrivaled knowledge of the sources of French institutional history, but he left only a large number of very brief studies of limited topics, many of which were published in the *Bulletin* of the Société d'Histoire Moderne and were never intended as a permanent record. Fortunately, many of these have been assembled and republished in a single volume. Among other things, Esmonin gives us an unusual glimpse of the operation of the royal councils, Louis

XIV's actual role in their deliberations, and how the ministers used the councils'—that is, the king's—authority to justify their actions. And in another earlier bit Esmonin reveals the strong influence of François de Harlay, Archbishop of Paris, upon the king in favor of the revocation of the Edict of Nantes. But these do scant justice to Esmonin's great knowledge of the period. As for Olivier-Martin, his ideas concerning French absolutism and institutions during Louis XIV's reign survive in extended form only in the mimeographed notes for his advanced courses. These are still authoritative but again very difficult to obtain. Truly the promise of French scholarship relative to Louis XIV's role as administrator fell far short of fulfillment. The advances that were made in this area must be distilled from the works on his more important aides, such as Colbert and Louvois.

One element of the French state system, however, was extensively elucidated at this time in C. G. Picavet, *La Diplomatie française au temps de Louis XIV*. This is a study of the mechanisms through which the Sun King's foreign policy was determined and made effective throughout Europe. The book examines the institutions and procedures of diplomacy at length as they functioned at this key moment, when French diplomats were considered to be the ablest in Europe and the system through which they operated attained its maximum development before the French Revolution. Picavet's study analyzes the many reforms that were instituted at this time, examines the functioning of the council of state, the secretary of state for foreign affairs, ambassadors and other personnel, and scrutinizes such matters as communications, declarations of war, treaties, the use of the French language in diplomacy, and many others. More general treatment is given the motives that underlay Louis XIV's foreign policy: the ideology of monarchy (especially Louis's idea of grandeur), economic factors, and public opinion. These, however, are merely listed without adequate integration into the functioning of the system. Throughout Picavet insists that Louis XIV, while necessarily relying upon the cooperation of his subordinates, was the prime mover in determining foreign policy and directing its implementation. Indeed, the entire mechanism was thoroughly centralized, and his control over the intricacies of negotiations was as effective as seventeenth-century conditions would permit. Thus the book, while adding little to knowledge of policy proper, explains in detail the means whereby it was effected and demonstrates the great extent to which the king's will was synonymous with French foreign relations in this crucial period.

Regarding the exact nature of Louis XIV's foreign policy, the most important revisionist contributions of the inter-war period were made by Gaston Zeller in a series of well-constructed and carefully documented articles which appeared in several different periodicals. First, he published a brief study showing the importance of Louvois's role in initiating the "reunions" which returned border territories to France beginning in 1679. In a lengthy commentary on Picavet's book, Zeller noted that the operations of the diplomatic system could hardly be understood without reference to the influence of key personalities, and he argued that Louis XIV's ideology of grandeur and corresponding objectives were fundamental motive-forces in the functioning of the diplomatic system. In fact, Zeller seemed to outdo Lavisse in stressing the king's mania for prestige and glory as determining the course of French foreign relations. Zeller then examined the long history of the attempts of the French kings to obtain the imperial crown and the title of emperor, showing that Louis XIV's efforts toward this end merely concluded a lengthy series of such maneuvers which extended over several centuries. And in 1933 and 1936 Zeller published two articles that were epoch-making in their way. These were devoted to the long-standing tradition that the French kings and their ministers consistently sought to extend the borders of the French kingdom to its "natural" frontiers: the Rhine boundary and the limits of ancient Gaul. Zeller examined the history of this concept, which we have noted in Lavisse, showing that it was generally accepted as historically accurate in modern French scholarship. He then proceeded to demolish it by examining the relevant sources and demonstrating that it was nonexistent as an objective of French foreign policy before the Revolution. The earlier kings and their ministers sought territorial expansion for strategic and prestige reasons, and only in the late eighteenth century did the idea of France's natural boundaries become a motive force in French diplomacy. This redefinition of the objectives of earlier French leaders, especially Richelieu and Louis XIV, has been thoroughly accepted and stands as one of the most successful revisionist efforts of the inter-war period.

In sum, the two decades between the two world wars witnessed certain advances in understanding Louis XIV and the nature of his reign, but contributions to knowledge were preponderantly along traditional lines, further elucidating matters whose importance had long been realized. Much remained to be done after the holocaust of World War II receded into the past and historians once more returned to their inquiries into the now distant reign of the Sun King.

DIVERSE CURRENTS SINCE WORLD WAR II

During the three decades since World War II, historical analysis of Louis XIV and his reign has expanded and deepened, producing many new approaches to the period and further insights into its nature and significance. Historical scholarship has been very rich and diverse, and the resulting contributions to knowledge have been unparalleled since the outburst of publication in the late nineteenth century. There are, however, marked differences between the efforts of recent historians and those of earlier periods. Publications of sources and multi-volume works has drastically decreased, their place being taken by shorter monographs and articles in historical periodicals, with only occasional works of synthesis, although the number of the latter is increasing. Also, it is apparent that many more non-French scholars are active in the field than previously. The most important development is undoubtedly the new attention that is given the other social sciences, particularly economics, sociology, and demography, with the all-important result that the emphasis has shifted from individuals—even the great and powerful, such as Louis XIV—to the broader context in which they lived. This fundamental reorientation has reached its culmination in the *Annales* school. Because of its special characteristics and great importance in the French wing of the historical profession, this school will be accorded individual treatment. Our approach to postwar historical scholarship will therefore be first to examine the many contributions of historians who are not members of the *Annales* school, after which we shall attempt to place this school in the general stream of scholarship on Louis XIV.

Continuing interest in Louis XIV as a person and as king is evidenced by the appearance of several biographies in the postwar period. Immediately in 1946, Auguste Bailly and Pierre Gaxotte issued lengthy and very laudatory accounts of the reign. Both authors make extensive use of memoirs and are very conscious of Louis XIV's greatness on all counts. Gaxotte, the abler of the two, did not hesitate to inject large elements of French patriotism into his narrative, praising Louis XIV's actions late in his reign, culminating in the Battle of Denain (1712), as saving France from her invading natural enemies, the Germans. Somewhat later, Vincent Cronin published a well-rounded biography of Louis XIV which focuses on the king and presents many insights into his age and motivation. All these works are designed for a wide reading audience and are successful in their way but present no new interpretations. The best biography of Louis XIV, however, is John B. Wolf's. This important work has all the assets of biography at its best: grace of style, expertise, and a sensitivity to the significance of large things and small. Wolf succeeds in placing the king in the context of his times by giving major attention to the wars which occupied so much of the reign. The narrative of these is the backbone of the book. The fact that the best available biography of Louis XIV—generally regarded as the greatest king of France—is the work of an American rather than a French historian is astonishing in itself but nevertheless true. It is one of many indications of the maturity of American scholarship and the prevailing tendency in France to discount the importance of individuals, however great.

Certain French authors nevertheless continue to manifest interest in the details of Louis XIV's personal life. In 1944 appeared Lieutenant Colonel Henri Carré's extensive work on the king's career to 1661. The emphasis of the book is upon the king's practical education, that is, his experiences early in life and the ways in which these molded his character and indicated growing maturity. These matters are also examined in Wolf's biography and his two chapters in John C. Rule's collection of essays, *Louis XIV and the Craft of Kingship,* where Wolf finds Louis's formal and practical education to have been both extensive and effective in determining his personal qualities and motivation. In addition, one of Jacques Saint-Germain's many works, *Louis XIV secret,* presents innumerable details concerning the king's private life, tastes, habits, and relations with those around him. Probably the most important lesson to be drawn from the book is the way in which all these features of Louis XIV's existence simply exuded his massive egotism, hauteur, and desire for domination of others. Saint-Germain's final chapter insists that, contrary to Saint-Simon's dictum, Louis XIV never rejected Paris and continued to lavish attention upon improving and embellishing the city, even after the building of Versailles, but Orest Ranum, in his *Paris in the Age of Absolutism* and a chapter in the Rule collection, and Leon Bernard, in his *The Emerging City: Paris in the Age of Louis XIV,* convincingly argue that most of the impetus and planning for these changes came from others, especially Colbert.

The royal court and Louis XIV's position in its midst, particularly after he took up residence at Versailles, continue to fascinate those who would understand the circumstances of the Sun King's life and motivation. The Duc de La Force, W. H. Lewis, and Gilette Ziegler have all published revealing and indeed fascinating studies of this phase of Louis XIV's existence, with much on daily life, ceremonial, personalities, and court intrigue. Little that is new is added by these books, although they serve to reemphasize these vital determinants in the king's life. Considerably more important regarding the impact of others upon Louis XIV's policies are recent efforts to fathom the motives and influence of the most enigmatical of his close associates, Madame de Maintenon. Louis Hastier's book does little but urge—rather unconvincingly—that she and Louis were married in 1697 rather than somewhere between 1683 and 1685. Jean Cordelier, however, has attempted a full-scale analysis of all phases of her career. His extensive study is well researched and presents a considerably more sympathetic picture of Madame de Maintenon than Langlois's earlier work, although recognizing her unlovable qualities. Cordelier not only analyzes the personal relationships of the king and his morganatic wife but presents insights into their attitudes, sentiments, and motives. He even extrapolates psychologically from a great variety of evidences and probably goes as far as is warranted in this respect. Regarding Madame de Maintenon's political influence, Cordelier insists that Louis discussed much with her, in part because he knew her to be more intelligent that he (an important judgment on Cordelier's part). Thus she knew many state secrets. But Louis always made the final decisions and indeed fended off pressures from all about him. Her influence slowly increased late in the reign, chiefly in religious affairs, but Cordelier is adamant that she had none concerning the revocation of the Edict of Nantes because this occurred before she had any political influence whatsoever. If she approved the action, she merely echoed general opinion at court. In matters of war and diplomacy she always favored peace and opposed all atrocities, thus finding herself disagreeing with Louvois. However, her weight in foreign affairs was extremely limited, and she had no connection with the policies that led to the War of the Spanish Succession. Cordelier's study therefore embodies important shifts of emphasis regarding Madame de Maintenon's exact role. While some of his methods and estimations may be questioned, he has provided the most thorough analysis of the problem to date.

Louis XIV's concept of kingship and the broader ideology of absolutism have been further elucidated in the postwar period by careful reexamination of a variety of sources. Regarding the king's understanding of his authority and its uses, the basic document is, of course, his *Memoirs for the Instruction of the Dauphin*. Bernard Champigneulles has published an uncritical edition of the memoirs, together with some of the king's other writings—his reflections on his *métier de roi*, his instructions to the Duc d'Anjou, many of his letters, and so on—making these readily available. The fundamental reanalysis of the nature and provenience of the memoirs, however, is the work of Paul Sonnino. In a key article in *French Historical Studies* and his introduction to his English translation of the memoirs, he rec-

tifies earlier ideas concerning their authorship and dates of
composition, and demonstrates that the king maintained close
supervision over their contents. Thus the memoirs may be relied
upon as firm evidence of Louis XIV's theoretical and at times
practical views of his God-given authority for absolute rule. Sonnino's edition is well indexed and is by far the most convenient
documentary source of Louis XIV's understanding of his profession of king.

Knowledge of the broader phases of royal absolutism, as it
was understood in Louis XIV's time, has also undergone further
refinement in a series of highly diverse but partially complementary publications. These include François Olivier-Martin's
important *Histoire du droit français,* sections of a book by Martin Göhring, several articles individually by Roland Mousnier
and Fritz Hartung and a very perceptive one that they constructed in concert, further articles centered upon Louis XIV's
ideology by François Dumont, Paul W. Fox, Herbert H. Rowen,
and Andrew Lossky, and most recently a full-scale examination
of Louis XIV's political ideas by Jean-Louis Thireau. These
studies, while not always in agreement, present innumerable
clarifications of the basic information in Lacour-Gayet's earlier
volume on the subject, too numerous to mention. The consensus
seems to be that absolutism in Louis XIV's time attributed "absolute" power to the sovereign in the following ways. He was
personally chosen by God to rule his subjects, held all necessary
authority, and enjoyed corresponding attributes and dignity.
He both led and symbolized the nation, and after his coronation was endowed with sacerdotal qualities. He alone held all
governmental power in the state, so that all acts of government
were done either by him in person or others acting in his name.
Although he was under great obligation to rule for the benefit
of his subjects, he was responsible only to God. All power and
majesty were therefore his, and his legitimate sphere of discre-
tion was correspondingly wide. On the other hand, this absolute
power suffered very real limitations. Being the fountain of justice, he was rightly obligated to observe the dictates of divine,
natural, and fundamental law, and at least in normal times
should respect the legal rights of his subjects, both individual
and corporate. No human agency, however, was empowered to

coerce the king to observe these important limitations on his power, and his subjects must unquestioningly obey, trusting in his superior wisdom and understanding of the mysteries of state. The latter position was greatly strengthened by the mystical elements of kingship which are extensively analyzed in Ernst Kantorowicz' monumental study, *The King's Two Bodies.* Although the book focuses more on England than the Continent and on the centuries before the seventeenth, it shows the roots and nature of this abstract but vital phase of kingship, which was still alive in Louis XIV's time.

The exact extent to which Louis XIV personally believed in absolutism thus defined has been carefully scrutinized by scholars, with varying results. While all agree that the Sun King accepted the major essentials of the position and strove throughout his reign to fulfill it to the utmost, scholars have disagreed concerning certain elements of his ideology and motivation. Thireau presents a systematic analysis of the doctrine of absolutism as of Louis XIV's time and finds evidence of *all* its essentials in the king's memoirs. And since Thireau, like Sonnino, believes that Louis was fully cognizant of their contents, he concludes that the king accepted the prevailing view of royal absolutism without major qualification. Fox, on the other hand, finds Louis XIV coming very close to Bodin's concept of despotism, although not outright tyranny. And Rowen, in a stimulating article in *French Historical Studies,* finds evidence that Louis XIV regarded the realm as his personal property, although in the special sense of early modern proprietary dynasticism. This position sharply qualifies that held by a majority of analysts. Regarding the trappings of monarchy and Louis XIV's concept of majesty, Mousnier insists—contrary to Lavisse—that these did not result from Spanish influence by Anne of Austria but were indigenous growths, quite in the nature of things in a regime of absolutism. On the other hand, Wolf strongly implies that Louis XIV may merely have tolerated the mystique of monarchy which was built up around him and was largely the work of others.

There is, furthermore, a fundamental divergence of opinion concerning the relevance of Louis XIV's ideas of glory and grandeur to his policies, particularly in the vital field of foreign affairs. Here there seems to be a remarkable difference of views between the French and the non-French authorities on the period. Generally, it appears that the ranking French historians —Mousnier, Tapié, Zeller, Goubert, and Mandrou—essentially cling to the position of Lavisse that Louis XIV's avid desire for glory and domination was a major, and on certain occasions *the* major, factor in impelling him into his many wars. On the other hand, British and American scholars—Wolf, Hatton, and Lossky—tend more to search for rational, positive explanations of his foreign policy at various points in his career and to discount emotional and ideological drives as determinative. This matter will be considered below in connection with the Sun King's diplomacy and wars. At this point it suffices to note this remarkable divergence of emphasis relative to motivational explanations. The difference may reflect the fact that British and American historians are capable of greater objectivity than the French when analyzing such matters. It may also indicate that the French historians are more sensitive and attuned to the broader implications, both theoretical and practical, of a ruler's lust for *gloire* and *grandeur*.

Louis XIVs work in reorganizing the royal administration and founding a genuine bureaucratic state continues to receive attention, although institutional history is very unfashionable at the present time in France. Lemontey's dictum that Louis XIV's major accomplishment was his work as administrator and that he thereby injected despotism into the fabric of the French governmental system was, as we have seen, taken up by Lavisse and Pagès, and continues to intrigue French historians. Mousnier, in his massive textbook, *Les XVIe et XVIIe siècles*, presents a variant of this position with certain important implications. He finds that Louis XIV, by using the royal councils, commissioners, intendants, and police, created a newly powerful, autocratic system which was so strong that it partially leveled the social pyramid and marked the transition to a new type of administrative state, altogether a revolutionary work. In addition, Mousnier has published many brief studies of governmental institutions, but these usually stop short in 1661. More recently, in conjunction with his extensive work on French social structure during the early modern period, he has shifted his exami-

nation of institutions from a more traditional analysis of their
structure, powers, and operations as functioning organisms to
their existence as component parts of organized society. In his
case, of course, these perspectives are mutually complementary
and represent a change of emphasis rather than a radical reorientation. Although Mousnier is not a member of the *Annales*
school, there is no doubt that his present approach to institutional history parallels this school's emphasis upon the study of
human activity in its total context. Indeed, Mousnier has been
in the forefront of those who have expanded knowledge of
social structure and its many ramifications in our period. His
present position is that institutions are groups of men who have
undertaken, or have been assigned to undertake, certain functions for the benefit of society, and that these institutions should
be understood in human terms through analysis of their members' total existence in society—their status, wealth, ideology,
and so on. For this purpose he edited a cooperative work, *Le
Conseil du roi, de Louis XII à la Révolution,* which analyzes
the social composition of the professional elements of the Council of State by assembling relevant statistics and examining the
education, ideals, and social and economic status of representative members, some of whom were active in the royal council
under Louis XIV. And most recently he has issued the first
volume of his monumental work of synthesis, *Les Institutions
de la France sous la monarchie absolue,* in which he develops
this approach to the study of institutions. All but the last two
chapters of this volume are devoted to the social foundations,
and only in the final portion does he initiate his examination of
the monarchical government. Here he focuses on the ideology
of absolute monarchy and the territorial, human, technological,
and financial circumstances that impinged upon its operations.
Again the contextual emphasis predominates. His specific treatment of actual institutions and their roles under Louis XIV's
leadership, however, must await further publication.

Paralleling the approach to institutional history that has been
developed by Mousnier and the *Annales* school, Julian Dent,
in his recent *Crisis in Finance: Crown, Financiers and Society
in Seventeenth-Century France,* analyzes, first, the organization
and functioning of the upper reaches of the royal financial ad-

ministration during the middle forty years of the century, and, second, the financiers as an element of French society. The book probes both matters more thoroughly than any earlier study, particularly in the areas of administrative practices and social dynamics, and starkly reveals the fundamental weaknesses of the royal financial system. After examining the established tax-collecting institutions and their procedures, Dent explores the *affaires extraordinaires,* that is, various forms of borrowing which involved committing future income. All responsible administrators, such as Colbert, hated these expedients but were forced to resort to them to meet the growing fiscal demands of the crown. The financiers, whom Dent defines as the men who handled royal money in their public and/or private capacities, in effect managed both ordinary and extraordinary sources of income and used established institutions as screens behind which to carry on their fraudulent self-enrichment. And Dent shows that the opportunities for this were extensive indeed. Although it was evident that corruption was widespread, reformers such as Colbert were quite unable to eliminate the abuses because there was no viable alternative system of administration and the king was absolutely dependent upon the financiers' cooperation to finance his increasingly costly projects. Thus the inefficiencies, peculations, and fiscal weaknesses of the crown continued unabated and became endemic in the monarchical system of government. In French society, however, the financiers had great difficulty in achieving respectability. They were resented for their ill-gotten wealth, their purchased patents of nobility, and the fact that, unlike the rest of the population, their upward social mobility was enhanced by adverse economic conditions and the king's mania for war. Although time and money enabled some families to gain a certain social standing, the position of the financiers remained precarious and they never acquired the corporate identity of so many groups above and below them in the social hierarchy.

Meanwhile, more traditional but equally important studies of individual institutions have made their appearance. The best analysis of Louis XIV's reorganization of the royal councils and their evolution throughout the reign since Boislisle's treatment of these matters is to be found in the introductory portion of

Michel Antoine's expert, exhaustive work, *Le Conseil du roi sous le règne de Louis XV*. Antoine traces the fundamental changes that were effected at once by Louis XIV and Colbert at the beginning of the king's personal reign, and shows how these reforms remained intact, with limited exceptions, to 1715— truly a major administrative accomplishment of great significance to effective royal power. Regarding the intendants, who were all-important arms of the monarchy in the provinces, Georges Livet and Henri Fréville have intensively studied the intendancies of Alsace and Brittany, and for the first time make available copious information on the functioning of these seeming viceroys. All elements of the topic are analyzed: their powers, policies, subordinates, reactions to local conditions, and the extent of their efficiency in their many undertakings. Inevitably, there was friction with the local authorities, especially in Alsace, where there were very unusual local factors, but the sum total of the intendants' activities hardly seems despotic. The third arm of the crown which Lemontey accused of despotism, the new Paris police, has been carefully examined in Jacques Saint-Germain's *La Reynie et la police au grand siècle*. This revealing treatment of La Reynie, the first lieutenant general of police in Paris and creator of the police system in the capital, is a remarkable study of its powers and functioning in a society that was quite unfamiliar with this type of regulation. When Saint-Germain describes the work of the police in reducing violence, aiding charitable activities, seeking to arrest prostitution, gambling, and the violation of sumptuary laws, controlling the press and booksellers, inspecting prisons, regulating economic matters, and implementing the revocation of the Edict of Nantes, our reaction is that these things were to be expected and must have been, in the main, beneficial to seventeenth-century Paris. Saint-Germain makes it clear, however, that La Reynie's police were generally hated by contemporaries because of friction with older bodies, the novelty of his methods, which were often high-handed, and his enforcement of regulations against all violators, including factious noblemen. When viewed in retrospect, the work of the royal councils, commissioners, intendants, and police seems to have been necessary to the building of the coming administrative state, but contemporaries could but view their acts as abusive innovations which frequently infringed upon traditional rights and privileges. For this reason, the historicist view would recognize a certain validity in Lemontey's charge that Louis XIV's reign marked the intrusion of despotism into the monarchical system of government.

Several additional suggestions concerning administrative developments in Louis XIV's reign have been advanced but await implementation. One of the potentially most fruitful is Ragnhild Hatton's thesis that the last generation of the reign witnessed major administrative reforms coupled with increased enlightenment in governmental matters, reflecting a new perception of the national interest. The proposal is well worth investigating and will doubtless provide valuable new insights into the realities of the period. The administrative aspect will be considered in Andrew Lossky's forthcoming book, *Louis XIV and the Ascendancy of France,* which will emphasize increasing governmental decentralization. Much evidence, however, must be examined before a comprehensive reinterpretation of this difficult period can be developed. Another valuable line of revisionist thought has been set forth by A. Lloyd Moote in an article in the *Journal of Modern History,* a chapter in the Rule collection of essays, and in the conclusion of his *Revolt of the Judges.* Moote argues that the Parlement of Paris did not lose all as a result of the Fronde, that it retained extensive influence in juridical, social, and economic matters, and that it even influenced political considerations throughout the reign. In other words, it retained a high degree of independence behind the façade of royal control and was always a factor to be dealt with in the formulation of official policy. There is much to be said for this position, provided that it is very carefully delineated, but it awaits demonstration which can only be based upon examination of a vast body of sources. On the other hand, one suggestion of earlier historians has been investigated and found wanting. This is the idea, which appears in so many overviews of the reign, that Louis XIV and Colbert attempted to rationalize the royal administration by applying the canons of Cartesian logic to governmental institutions and practices. James E. King's book investigates this proposition and assembles a mass of purported evidence in support of it, but the effort is unconvincing because it fails to demonstrate that king and minister went any further in their Cartesianism than common-sense measures for increased order and efficiency.

Nothing illustrates more vividly the orientation of postwar French historians away from outstanding individuals than the lack of attention to Louis XIV's greatest ministers, Colbert and Louvois. Neither has received a full-scale treatment since the works of Cole and Boissonnade on Colbert and Louis André on Louvois, and these date from the inter-war period. This neglect of key personalities seems to stem more from a reorientation of historical perspectives than satisfaction with these earlier works, if recent criticisms of Cole and Boissonnade by members of the *Annales* school are indicative. Be that as it may, the postwar period has witnessed extremely little publication on either Colbert or Louvois. Georges Mongrédien's *Colbert* presents much interesting information, but his intent is to discover the man behind the minister rather than his official activities. The more human side of Colbert he ably analyzes, including his relations with his sovereign, but he goes no further. Andrew Lossky's forthcoming work, however, will include an analysis of Colbert's system. Because of the *Annales* school's great interest in economic history, several of its members have examined Colbert's work, as will be indicated below, but their efforts have been limited to summaries and reinterpretations of his activities in the context of broader economic currents. As for Louvois, the great neglect of both military and diplomatic history in France doubtless accounts for the lack of interest in his career. Only a valuable, wide-ranging selection of his letters has been published by Jacques Hardré in the postwar period, and this in the United States. And the exact relationships between Louis XIV and his ministers are as uncertain as ever. Mousnier has adhered to the traditional position that Louis closely controlled their activities, both by close surveillance and by fostering rivalry between the Colbert and Le Tellier families, whereas Wolf and several others see Louis habitually resorting to team efforts which allowed his subordinates much latitude and practical influence. Again more precise measurements seem to be needed.

The changed perspective in historians' approach to Louis

XIV's reign are nowhere more evident than in their analyses of the evolution of French society. In 1945, Philippe Sagnac published a general work of synthesis, *La Formation de la société française moderne,* the first volume of which traces the social changes in France under Louis XIV. Here Sagnac essentially accepts and builds upon Lavisse's assumption that the great determinant in effecting social change was royal policy. Sagnac consequently examines the evolution of the nobles, clergy, jurists, bourgeoisie, and peasants (the traditional categories) from this standpoint, tracing their increased subjection to governmental controls and exploitation, and the deterioration of the position of all save those of highest rank in the latter part of the reign. Since Sagnac's book, students of French society have largely moved away from this government-centered approach to social change and have studied the elements of French society more as living entities with their own dynamics. To be sure, a few have continued to examine the impact of royal policy upon various groups. In 1960, Eugene L. Asher published *The Resistance of the Maritime Classes,* which examines the opposition to Colbert's efforts to recruit the needed personnel for his new navy. And in the same year R. B. Grassby published an important article in the *Economic History Review,* entitled "Social Status and Commercial Enterprise under Louis XIV." This valuable study examines the efforts of the king and his aides to create a *noblesse commerçante,* particularly during the latter part of the reign, by granting various privileges and protection against derogation. The effort, however, failed both because of the opposition of the nobility and the merchants, whose ingrained habits and social values were offended, and because the crown gave only half-hearted support to measures that would have compromised its interests if the structure of French society had been significantly altered.

Such studies are the exception, however, because of the massive shift of emphasis to social structure as a field of research. An early instance of this is François Olivier-Martin's juridical study, *L'Organisation corporative de la France d'ancien régime.* Since World War II, analyses of French social structure have proliferated by leaps and bounds, largely under the leadership of the *Annales* school. These are far too numerous to men-

tion and in any case have little to do with Louis XIV. Among
the most active contributors to knowledge of French society in
all its aspects, however, Roland Mousnier is without peer. His
studies are usually broader than those of the *Annales* school and
embody the fruits of his enormously extensive investigations.
These may be said to culminate in the first volume of his *Institutions de la France sous la monarchie absolue,* which has been
cited above. In his studies of the relationships of the various
orders, estates, and other groupings with the royal government,
Mousnier approaches the matter from two different perspectives. One is the manner and extent to which these groups par-
ticipated in the royal administration. This is the subject of the
volume *Le Conseil du roi,* which he edited, his study of the
maîtres des requêtes in his *Lettres et mémoires adressés au chancelier Séguier,* and several essays in *La Plume, la faucille et le
marteau.* Another example of inquiry into the participation of
certain social entities in government is the special, cooperative
issue of *XVIIe Siècle,* which examines the social origins of the
holders of several types of offices. These studies throw much
light not upon royal subordination of French society but rather
the reverse—an important corrective to the position of Lavisse
and Sagnac, since it is thereby made clear that Louis XIV's policies involved much more than subjugation and exploitation. The
impact of royal policy upon French society, however, should
not be forgotten, and Mousnier will doubtless analyze this and
much more in additional volumes of his *Institutions de la France
sous la monarchie absolue.* In the interim, the direction of his
thought may be gleaned from the notes for his course at the
Sorbonne, *État et société sous François Ier et pendant le gouvernement personnel de Louis XIV.*

One important element of French social history that is relevant to Louis XIV's policies has been superficially examined by
scholars but awaits adequate treatment. The importance of
peasant uprisings during the seventeenth century, primarily
against royal fiscality, was first emphasized by Lavisse and
Pagès but has received extensive investigation only since World
War II. Unfortunately, almost all these studies focus on the
upheavals that occurred before 1661, the area of the resounding
Mousnier-Porchnev debate. The uprisings during Louis XIV's

personal reign ended for all intents and purposes with that in Brittany in 1675. These have been sketched by Leon Bernard in an article in *French Historical Studies,* which supports Porchnev in part, and Mousnier has analyzed the Breton insurrection of 1675 in his *Fureurs paysannes.* The most extensive recent treatment of the latter is *Les Révoltes bretonnes de 1675: Papier timbré et bonnets rouges,* by Yvon Garlan and Claude Nières. This small volume traces the many elements of the rebellion by quoting at length from contemporary memoirs, documents, and other sources, and vividly reveals the motives that led urban and rural Bretons to resort to force against Colbert's efforts to wring new levies from the province. When analyzing the social significance of the movement, Garlan and Nières lean strongly toward Porchnev's Marxian confrontation of classes, especially as this appeared in rural southern Brittany. The book, however, provides no solution to the very important question why this was the last major rebellion of this type against governmental authority during Louis XIV's reign after their endemic persistence throughout the entire previous three-quarters of the century. Was it because of royal policy, changes in French society, or a combination of these? Mousnier offers certain tentative explanations based on evolving social structure, recruitment of great numbers of men for the army and the police, and the growing power of the intendants, while Le Roy Ladurie, a leader of the *Annales* school, adds several further considerations: Colbert's reduction of thefts from the lower classes by the tax collectors and his replacing direct taxes with indirect, the intendants' greater efforts to defend the local population against exploitation by agents of the crown and neighboring landlords, the increased loyalism of the Catholic masses which resulted from the persecution of the Huguenots, and the general decline of violence and criminality. But these authors and John H. M. Salmon, who has commented on the matter, would be the first to admit that the whole phenomenon of popular unrest in Louis XIV's personal reign needs further research, particularly as it was related to royal policies.

Unlike recent treatments of institutional and social history, investigations of Louis XIV's policies relative to religious issues have continued essentially along traditional lines, their authors merely seeking further elucidation of issues and episodes whose importance has long been recognized. As yet, there is no general work of synthesis which demonstrates the great importance of religious factors to many of the Sun King's policies, although Lossky's forthcoming work promises consideration of this vital matter, and Bruno Neveu's excellent edition of the *Correspondance du nonce en France Angelo Ranuzzi (1683–1689)* provides valuable insights into the manifold complexities of church-state relations during this crucial period. Louis XIV's highly personalized approach to the papacy has recently been analyzed in several studies. Paul Sonnino's *Louis XIV's View of the Papacy (1661–1667)* shows how the young king, while not entirely unconcerned, was thoroughly contemptuous of the papacy during the early years of his reign and felt that he could easily ignore or override it. The most intensive examinations of king-pope relations, however, have centered upon the climax of their differences: the all-out struggle between Louis XIV and Innocent XI. The moment is revealing in many ways, since the Sun King was at the height of his power and Innocent XI, the so-called Jansenist pope, was a model of papal intransigence. Jean Orcibal and André Latreille have published two thorough, complementary studies which elucidate the extremely intricate factors that produced the impasse. Orcibal examines the events that led to the excommunication of Louis XIV and his ministers in 1688, after which Louis appealed from the papal actions to a future council, thereby challenging the supremacy of the papacy itself. Orcibal then asks why the threatened schism never occurred and finds an explanation in the pressure of opinion in many important quarters plus the king's unwillingness to push the matter to unnecessary extremes. Latreille focuses upon Innocent XI's psychology and presents a revealing analysis of his ideology and motivation, which led to confrontations that could be resolved only by his death. Although limited, both studies are expert and valuable contributions of the type that is very much needed in this field.

Gallicanism was a major issue throughout Louis XIV's reign and has been studied by a few scholars. Pierre Blet's careful examination of the Assembly of the Clergy shows how the king early in his personal reign maintained traditional relations with that body while simultaneously moving to strengthen the crown's position regarding the *don gratuit,* jurisdiction, and the *régale.* The ablest recent student of French Gallicanism is Aimé-Georges Martimort, whose masterpiece, *Le Gallicanisme de Bossuet,* is broader than its title indicates and examines Gallicanism throughout most of the century. Understandably, the work focuses on Bossuet, but it gives much information on the cooperation of king and bishop, especially relative to the Four Articles of 1682. More tangential to royal policy is Raymond Schmittlein's extensive, polemical work on the *différend* between Bossuet and Fénelon. The quietist controversy and relevant intrigues are here examined in a manner very hostile to Bossuet, but the king is only a shadowy figure in the background. Regarding the thorny problems that Jansenism presented to Louis XIV, only limited additions to knowledge have been made. Antoine Adam and Louis Cognet have produced excellent but very brief works of synthesis, and René Taveneaux has published many documents illustrative of the struggle between the king and this very obdurate sect. All these authors, plus Jacques-François Thomas in a full-scale treatment, give attention to the bull *Unigenitus* and its disruptive aftermath, incidentally revealing much concerning Louis XIV's reasons for attempting to extirpate Jansenism. His exact role in each episode, however, has yet to be determined. Again it is the critical question of the king's relations with his advisers. The focus of all these authors upon other personalities—and the same is true of J. G. Judge's able, incisive essay in the Rule collection—implies that the influence of such key figures as Bossuet, Harlay de Champvallon, and Madame de Maintenon was often determinative. But this difficult matter awaits further elucidation.

Unlike Louis XIV's policies relative to the Catholic majority of his subjects and church-state relations, his persecution of the Huguenots and revocation of the Edict of Nantes have received such expert treatment that a certain consensus of opinion has emerged. This is largely due to Jean Orcibal's excellent book, *Louis XIV et les protestants,* which, in fact, is closely followed by all later writers on the subject. Here Orcibal expertly reviews all major elements of this dramatic phase of the Sun King's religious policy: early efforts toward reunion of churches, the

caisse des conversions, the *dragonnades,* the king's reasons for
seeking religious uniformity, the revocation, and its compli-
cated aftermath in the years which also witnessed the beginnings of the Enlightenment. Orcibal's documentation of his
views on these matters is so thorough that they seem impossible
to challenge. Regarding Louis XIV's exact role and motivation,
not only Orcibal but the historian of Protestanism, Emile G.
Léonard, and Daniel Robert in a carefully constructed article
agree that the king sought religious unity not for religious reasons but political: his dislike of division within the realm and
especially the evolution of the foreign situation in the 1680s.
They also agree that the policy was completely the king's, that
he knew of all essential developments including the use of
force, that others in his entourage had only minimal direct
influence upon his actions, and that he consistently pursued an
anti-Huguenot policy which varied only in its implementation
according to circumstances. Ragnhild Hatton adds that Louis
XIV was naturally tolerant and would have preferred less co-
ercive measures, and Pierre Chaunu agrees, speculating that
these might in fact have succeeded and that the revocation,
which was contrary to the king's nature, actually restored life
to French Protestantism, which was slowly dying because of
internal institutional and doctrinal difficulties. The picture that
emerges seems clear and places primary responsibility upon the
king, who, however, acted in a complex, evolving situation
which pushed him to take the fatal step. As for its impact upon
France, all agree that its effect was deleterious in foreign affairs,
but Warren C. Scoville has successfully demonstrated that its
great adverse influence upon the French economy—an article
of faith among historians since Voltaire—has been greatly exaggerated. Scoville reviews the problem industry by industry
and shows that except in a few instances the major causes of
decline lay elsewhere, chiefly the impact of Louis XIV's wars
and broader economic currents. Scoville's work is outstanding
as one of the most successful pieces of historical revisionism by
an American scholar.

The great significance of Louis XIV's foreign policy and wars
has long been recognized and continues to attract the attention of scholars although in a very unusual pattern, since it is

in this area of research that the work of non-French historians is most evident. More than any other aspect of Louis XIV's reign, his foreign policy has become the subject of investigation by American, British, and German historians, and it is they who have made the most recent contributions to knowledge. The decline of interest in this field in France is generally recognized, and not the least of its causes is the hostility of the *Annales* school to diplomatic history, which many of its members view as the prize example of historical writing that unduly neglects the broader context in which events occur. Diplomatic history is not extinct in France—witness the continued success of the *Revue d'histoire diplomatique* under the capable guidance of Georges Dethan—but studies of Louis XIV's reign in this periodical are rare. The continuing publication of the important *Recueil des instructions données aux ambassadeurs et ministres de France depuis les traités de Westphalie jusqu'à la révolution française* provides additional source material. Nevertheless, it is true that the major new perspectives in this field have been developed outside of France. Among the more important German contributions to the field, Heinrich von Srbik's *Wien und Versailles, 1692–1697* and especially Max Braubach's *Versailles und Wien von Ludwig XIV bis Kaunitz* may be noted. The many publications on specific elements of Louis XIV's foreign policy are too numerous to be examined here and are listed in any comprehensive bibliography of the reign; that in John C. Rule's *Louis XIV and the Craft of Kingship* is one of the best. Our intention is merely to indicate the more important interpretations of Louis XIV's exact role, methods, motivation, and objectives in this crucial phase of his leadership of France.

Early in the postwar period there appeared three general works of synthesis on Louis XIV's foreign policy: Louis André's *Louis XIV et l'Europe*, Jacques Droz's *Histoire diplomatique de 1648 à 1789*, and Gaston Zeller's *Histoire des relations internationales*, Vol. III[2]: *De Louis XIV à 1919*. All summarize generally accepted historical information and agree that Louis XIV personally directed his foreign policy and assumed all responsibility, that he pursued no consistent program such as the Spanish succession or the attainment of France's natural boundaries, and that he was always pragmatic in his approach to policy, although very concerned about France's northern and eastern frontiers. They also agree that Louis was greatly pre-occupied with his personal glory, that he viewed war as a legit-imate means of increasing his prestige both at home and abroad, and that he thoroughly confused his personal interests and grandeur with those of the nation. They disagree, however, con-cerning the exact extent to which his desire for glory and domi-nance determined his foreign policy and precipitated his wars. Louis André presents the most circumspect picture, showing that the Sun King's penchant for greatness in the eyes of all was frequently and increasingly moderated by circumstances as the reign progressed. Jacques Droz calls Louis's quest for glory the leitmotiv of the reign, although he too finds greater moderation on the king's part in its last generation. It is Zeller who is most adamant in demonstrating that Louis XIV's primary motiva-tion was his search for personal glory. In this work and his chap-ter in the fifth volume of the *New Cambridge Modern History,* Zeller specifically states this to have been the king's principal stimulus and that he measured all opportunities in foreign affairs from this standpoint. "The first objective of Louis XIV—one may say his permanent objective—in foreign enterprises was to acquire 'glory.' " And Zeller treats all major episodes of the reign accordingly, stressing the king's brutal tactics and domineering attitude toward friend and foe alike. Not all blame, says Zeller, should fall upon the king, since he was strongly influenced by others—by Colbert in initiating the Dutch War and even more so by Louvois in all his violent, predatory moves in the 1680s— but the king always retained close supervision and was entirely aware of all that occurred. Zeller even implies that Louis XIV's aggressive, domineering attitude remained unchanged through-out the entire reign, consistent to the end.

None of these works made any genuine contribution to knowledge of Louis XIV's foreign policies or was intended to. After their appearance, however, publications on Louis XIV's conduct of foreign affairs sharply diminished. The few authori-tative, insightful studies that appeared in the 1960s were usually in the form of brief essays on specific topics. An example is the valuable collection in the special issue of *XVIIe Siècle* entitled

"Problèmes de politique étrangère." For our purposes, the most significant of these is the essay by Victor-L. Tapié plus two others that he published elsewhere: "Europe et chrétienté. Idée chrétienne et gloire dynastique dans la politique européenne au moment du siège de Vienne (1683)," in *Gregorianum*, and "Nec pluribus impar," in *La France au temps de Louis XIV*. In these brief but cogent pieces, Tapié sets forth views of major importance concerning the Sun King's motivation and objectives. Recognizing that the king's pursuit of glory was undoubtedly one of the constants of the period, Tapié reminds us that Louis XIV believed glory and renown might be attained through a variety of means, of which war was but one, although one of the most fruitful. More important, in all these essays Tapié strongly presses his conviction that the 1680s represent the worst period of Louis XIV's reign for a variety of reasons. Not only did his aggressiveness, intolerance, and use of terror under Louvois's baneful influence reach their climax; the king also seemed to lose sight of the true interests of the various states, so bent was he upon pursuing his goal of domination. Most significant of all, in Tapié's eyes, was his failure to aid the Christian forces during the siege of Vienna. The idea of Christendom was still very much alive, he recalls, and Louis XIV, the Most Christian King and Eldest Son of the Church, should have sent reinforcements to the hastily assembled Christian army which successfully resisted the assault of the infidel. Instead, the Sun King at the height of his power continued to pursue dynastic advantage in the west by acts of aggression against border territories, thereby divorcing himself and his cause from Christian ideals. The result was that the Emperor assumed leadership of Christian Europe, and French dynastic prestige came to be associated with mere dominance and gain—a vital equation which had far-reaching consequences. The subsequent war pitted France against almost all Europe, and the balance of power inexorably shifted away from France. Tapié admits that the last years of the reign witnessed a much more moderate Louis XIV, chastened by reverses and having learned from experience. His more enlightened policies finally extricated France from the final conflict in the reign and preserved her position in the new balance of power.

Meanwhile a number of American and British historians have been developing new perspectives on Louis XIV's foreign policy. An early instance of this in the postwar period is Herbert H. Rowen's study, *The Ambassador Prepares for War: The Dutch Embassy of Arnauld de Pomponne, 1669–1671.* Here Rowen analyzes French diplomacy in preparation for the assault on the Dutch which began in 1672. He concludes that the essential issues at stake were diplomatic rather than economic and presents a strong case for this, contrary to the usual position that Colbert's support of the war against the commercially powerful Dutch was a major factor in causing the conflict. While Colbert's precise influence at this point—a very difficult matter to demonstrate—has yet to be established, Rowen's book is a valuable contribution. Much more controversial is the picture of Louis XIV that Stephen B. Baxter draws in his *William III.* In discussing the intense rivalry of these two key figures, particularly during the crucial 1680s, Baxter presents Louis XIV as brutal, tyrannical, and persecuting, overriding both friend and foe, and repeatedly violating the principles of international law. The 1680s may have witnessed many questionable acts on the part of the Grand Monarch, but Baxter's description is surely overdrawn and cannot be accepted by historians who view events from the French side of the English Channel.

For some years, Andrew Lossky has been studying the elements of Louis XIV's political ideology and the ways in which it influenced and is visible in his foreign policy. Lossky's findings are set forth in three important essays in as many different collections: *The Responsibility of Power,* edited by Krieger and Stern, *William III and Louis XIV,* edited by Hatton and Bromley, and *Louis XIV and the Craft of Kingship,* edited by John C. Rule. In these solid and well-constructed pieces, Lossky develops certain themes which have direct relevance to the king's direction of foreign affairs. He shows that Louis XIV held to an orthodox but relatively unsophisticated version of divine-right absolutism, buttressed by a thoroughly pessimistic view of human nature which therefore required strong controls. As for his views that affected his relations with other states, Lossky approaches this important matter not from the usual standpoint—Louis XIV's avid desire for glory—but according to his belief in certain more practical constants. The king, he shows, held that a divinely established natural order prevailed among states, strictly hierarchical in nature with absolute monarchy the best and most efficient, and that each state, because of its nature, had certain characteristic interests. The result was that Louis XIV held to certain "true maxims of state" which partially guided his foreign policy. Although Louis XIV was always pragmatic in meeting given situations, Lossky shows how these maxims were either insightful or misleading on many occasions. In fact, he divides the reign into nine different periods when the king followed these constants and other elements of his thought to varying degrees, as evidenced by his stated views and/or actual policies. From this standpoint, it is interesting to note, he finds the nadir of the reign in the 1680s, when the Sun King significantly departed from his maxims and instead indulged in shortsighted, irrational acts of violence which seem to reflect sheer confusion and emotional outbursts on his part. Louvois's influence was partially to blame, Lossky contends, but the king was unable to disembarrass himself of his war minister until the latter's death in 1691. The approach is fruitful and provides additional insights into Louis XIV's all-important direction of foreign affairs. It will undoubtedly receive further development in Lossky's projected volume on the entire reign.

Lossky has also carefully studied the mechanisms and objectives of French foreign policy during the last generation of the reign in his contribution to the sixth volume of the *New Cambridge Modern History*. He shows that in this period Louis again was guided in part by his maxims of state and that he genuinely worked for a balance of power, especially in the early years of the eighteenth century. For this he developed efficient procedures and indulged in much careful planning, resulting in statesmanship of a high order. More on this also may be expected in his forthcoming book. In fact, French foreign relations during the final portion of the reign have received expert new treatment in several quarters. John C. Rule has published two valuable essays on Colbert de Torcy, again as part of his preparation of a full-scale study of this very important foreign minister. These are to be found in the Hatton and Bromley collection, mentioned above, and *Studies in Diplomatic History,* edited by Hatton and Anderson. In these perceptive studies, Rule traces Torcy's working relationship with Louis XIV during the War of the Spanish Succession in such a way as to clarify the role of both parties. It has long been known that Torcy was the most influential minister in this dramatic portion of the reign, but no adequate analysis of his activities is available. Rule's book will surely fill this gap and will provide much information on the perennial question of Louis XIV's relations with his ministers and the exact extent of their influence upon policy. Also it should be noted that the late Mark A. Thomson produced several very closely reasoned studies of various elements of French foreign policy in this period. Three of particular note are reproduced in the Hatton and Bromley collection. These are "Louis XIV and William III, 1689–1697," which is epoch-making in its way, "Louis XIV and the Origins of the War of the Spanish Succession," which is especially noteworthy for its insights into the king's state of mind in the crucial opening years of the eighteenth century, and "Louis XIV and the Grand Alliance, 1705–1710," which traces the tortuous but revealing negotiations and Louis's abortive efforts for peace to 1710. These are exactly the type of analysis that is needed for the reinterpretation of Louis XIV's last years which seems to be in the making.

It is Ragnhild Hatton who has made the most extensive revisionist proposals relative to the last generation of Louis XIV's reign. Her view that the period witnessed significant administrative reforms and a new spirit of enlightenment has been referred to above. In the field of foreign policy her suggestions are equally sweeping. Basing her conception largely upon her extensive study of diplomacy, she would depict a rather different Louis XIV, more the experienced, high-minded, conciliatory leader than the usual portrait of the aging autocrat stubbornly maintaining his resolve and demonstrating a certain greatness in the midst of reverses. This view of the Sun King she sets forth especially in three publications, her essay in the Rule collection, her *Louis XIV and His World,* and a recent article in the *Journal of Modern History*—all very perceptive and authoritative studies. Although aware of the king's latent penchant for personal glory, she emphasizes instead his methods, attitudes, and objectives as these are evidenced in his conduct of foreign relations, thereby uncovering a much more moderate and responsible Louis XIV than appears in most French publications. The Sun King's bad press, she claims, stems largely from legend which is now being discarded. Admitting that the War of Devolution and the Dutch War were aggressive in nature and did not produce the expected gains, she urges that Louis XIV learned extensively from experience and rarely overreached himself later. Even his acts of violence in the 1680s, such as the bombardment of Genoa and the devastation of the Palatinate, had their rational explanations in the diplomatic situation and the usages of war, she says, obviously differing from such authors as Tapié, who would give the period an entirely different complexion. The result was that the mature Louis XIV who faced the problem of the Spanish succession showed himself to be moderate in his demands and responsible in negotiation, adhering to his code of honor yet readily making concessions. Far from merely pursuing dynastic advantage, Louis XIV had the true interests of the nation at heart and ultimately succeeded in defending them in the face of great odds.

In this sympathetic portrayal, Louis XIV becomes the enlightened, experienced statesman who was characterized by moderation and responsibility rather than the egocentric, domineering autocrat whose wars bled the nation white for purposes of dynastic advantage and prestige. And this altered picture of the aging Louis XIV is based upon extensive research which will provide the foundation of a significantly revised interpretation of the final generation of the reign. This process of rectification, however, may be pushed too far, as Professor Hatton admits, since Louis XIV remained arbitrary and autocratic in many things to the end. In this regard, it may not be inappropriate to note that all these leading investigators who support this altered view of the later Louis XIV—Hatton, Thomson, Lossky, Rule—have approached the period through the study of diplomatic history. In this area there is undoubtedly need for extensive revision, but the question is how far the image of the sovereign should be altered. The study of diplomatic history finely reveals the methods, attitudes, and objectives of its participants, but it often leaves the latent assumptions and broader context hidden. It may also provide few guides to emotional factors, such as Louis XIV's vision of glory and the clash of values, that were associated with events. And, most important, by providing rational, pragmatic explanations of policy, it may justify through hindsight much that was quite unjustified in the eyes of contemporaries. Present-day scholars know immeasurably more about the intricacies of Louis XIV's foreign policy than did all but a few around him, yet all of his contemporaries were in contact with thousands of facets of life that will never be known to later researchers, and they had the inestimable advantage of sharing with their sovereign the prevailing values of their time. These advantages of contemporaries should not be taken lightly in any historical revisionism and seem especially pertinent when studying such a complex period as the last generation of Louis XIV's reign. Certainly the criticisms of Louis XIV by such astute observers as Vauban, Fénelon, even Saint-Simon and certain others should not be casually discarded. A new and very significant interpretation of this period of French history is undoubtedly in the making, but the revised picture of Louis XIV should take account of the views of his critics who knew him as no historian can.

That Louis XIV inflicted much suffering upon his realm during his later years and left governmental finance in complete disorder when he died is still accepted by most historians. Although recent scholarship places more emphasis upon the broad adverse trends in the European economy and less upon the king's responsibility, it remains clear that the widespread misery in France during this period was in part due to royal policies, especially the incessant wars. An examination of the writings of such different authors as Warren C. Scoville, whose book on the economic impact of the Huguenot exodus has been mentioned above, and Jean Meuvret, in his chapter in the *New Cambridge Modern History* and some of his collected essays, at least demonstrates agreement on this fundamental point. And the chaos in governmental finance is undeniable. Jacques Saint-Germain's books on Paul Poisson de Bourvalais and Samuel Bernard, and the much more scholarly work of Herbert Lüthy, *La Banque protestante en France*, give graphic descriptions of the incredible measures that Louis XIV's finance ministers were forced to adopt and the essential bankruptcy of the royal government at the end of the reign. As for the many high-ranking critics of royal policy, however, only slight additions to knowledge have been made. The strictures of Fénelon, Vauban, Saint-Simon, Boisguillebert, and many others have been known so long that little need be added. Lionel Rothkrug's *Opposition to Louis XIV* is not as comprehensive as its title suggests and develops certain themes, chiefly in economic theory, broadly defined. Mousnier has conveniently put together much information on Vauban's major economic work in the notes for his course, *La Dîme de Vauban*. Regarding Fénelon, Mousnier has taken an unusual position in the generally laudatory literature on the famous archbishop. His article in the commemorative issue of *XVIIe Siècle* (reproduced in *La Plume, la faucille et le marteau*) revives the idea that Fénelon's criticisms of Louis XIV were inappropriate because he looked backward in time and argued essentially from religious morality without regard for contemporary conditions. When Fénelon advocated reviving the nobility, reducing the burden of government, and maintaining the peace of Europe, he was quite unaware of such fundamental facts as the changes in French society, the growth of the administrative state, and the threats to France's existence from abroad. His political ideas were therefore both retrograde and utopian. Whether Mousnier's observations, which are obviously based on a knowledge of future developments, entirely discredit Fénelon's criticisms of Louis XIV's policies as they were viewed in his own time may be debated. Françoise Gallouédec-Genuys has given us a full-scale exposition of Fénelon's political philosophy and has succeeded in showing that it embodied much that was best in the thought of the period.

It should be clear from this survey that the postwar years have witnessed anything but unanimity among historians concerning Louis XIV's place in history. Disagreement regarding much that is fundamental remains the order of the day, perhaps more so than at any other time. New perspectives have been developed and much excellent research accomplished, adding significantly to our body of knowledge, but many of the recently advanced views have yet to be substantiated before they are incorporated into the accepted body of scholarship. As always, the richer the inquiry, the more diverse the conclusions. It remains to be examined whether the *Annales* school, so predominant in France, has provided satisfactory answers to some of the current outstanding questions.

THE ANNALES SCHOOL

The large and influential group of French historians who are generally known as the *Annales* school enjoys a commanding position in the profession in France today. The story of the founding and expansion of this school has been repeatedly told and can easily be read in the accounts of Jean Glénisson and Jack Hexter: how during the inter-war years Marc Bloch and Lucien Febvre, then at Strasbourg, rejected traditional, empirical history, which stressed persons, events, and institutions, and advocated that human phenomena be studied in their economic, social, and psychological context; how they founded their mouthpiece, the *Annales: Economies, sociétés, civilisations* (its title since 1946), which gave the school its name; how its base of operations was established in the VIe Section of the École Pratique des Hautes Études in Paris; and how it expanded to a position of predominance in the historical profession. There can be no doubt concerning its significance or its impact. Its challenge to traditional history has been so thorough and successful that even the ranking French authorities in such fields as institutional and diplomatic history have adopted many of its precepts. And its influence outside France is strong and increasing. Furthermore, no major countercurrent among French historians is visible and, indeed, none seems likely in the near future because of the prominence of the *Annales* school in the profession, its claim to "total" history as its purview, and its ability to absorb—or at least to pigeonhole —all new contributions to historical knowledge. It is fitting, therefore, to examine its precepts and publications relative to Louis XIV in terminating this survey.

The philosophy of the *Annales* school—for it has a philosophy despite repeated disclaimers—has been described by II. R. Trevor-Roper as "social determinism with a difference." That the predominant school of historical research in France, whose citizens have always prided themselves on their individuality, should espouse a deterministic philosophy is surprising and may partially account for the failure of the school to achieve a wide, enthusiastic following among the *grand public*. The obvious question that Trevor-Roper's statement raises, however, is the extent to which the "difference" qualifies the thoroughly deterministic position that the school has adopted. Trevor-Roper says that it is "limited and qualified by recognition of independent human vitality." Exactly what this means is not clear, and in any case it undoubtedly differs among many members of the school. An examination of their treatment of Louis XIV—certainly one of the most vital personages in French history—should provide certain answers to this question while detailing their contributions to knowledge of his reign. But first we should glance at the methods and assumptions of the *Annales* school.

The stated objective of this school is to understand the totality of human history by applying a sophisticated interdisciplinary methodology to the study of human society. For this purpose they attempt to elucidate the innumerable elements of, and factors that impinge upon, the structure and functioning of society by maximum utilization of the various social sciences. Although the spectrum is "total," the position rests upon the assumption that the contextual element in human affairs is the most fundamental and therefore in large measure determinative. And varying degrees of success have attended the borrowings from other social sciences in their historical dimension. The clearest successes have been registered in the study of economic and sociological phenomena, separately and in combination. Sophisticated statistical techniques have enabled such authorities as Jean Meuvret to reveal much concerning the economy of seventeenth-century France, especially through investigation of price cycles. And demographic studies of a statistical nature have given powerful assistance to analysis of the society of the period. The extremely complex, hierarchical, and corporate society that prevailed in France has been examined in great detail through extensive examination of its various elements. Much has been learned about the all-important societal framework within which all human activity occurred, although attention has inevitably focused upon the group rather than the individual. The latter, in fact, is usually treated simply as a member of a group with common interests, characteristics, and activities, and it has even been suggested that models may be developed to facilitate this type of historical investigation. These economic and sociological studies are obviously interrelated and in combination have expanded our understanding of the structure and functioning of French society as never before. They thereby have added greatly to historical knowledge, although the focus and methodology frequently cause the individual to be lost in the collectivity. In addition, the psychological dimension of human activity has been investigated from the standpoint of collective mentality, although with considerably less success than the economic and social. This is doubtless because intangibles are much less susceptible of statistical analysis and must, at least in part, be handled in an impressionistic manner which the rigorists of the school instinctively reject. Although much is known concerning the ideological, religious, and sentimental precepts of the period, much remains to be done to develop this area of contextual analysis.

The dynamics of all these factors are central to their historical significance and have received corresponding attention from the *Annales* school. Here we meet their favorite terms: *"conjonctures"* (an untranslatable term variously meaning situation, transformation, change, curves, cycles, rhythm) and *"structures,"* denoting elements that make for continuity or slow change. Both are used in the investigation of many fields, although the former is especially appropriate to the economic and the latter to the social and institutional. The fundamental assumption is that the innumerable contextual factors which constantly impinge upon human activity occur and evolve at extremely different rates, some in a moment whereas others, such as climate, change slowly through an entire millennium. And all but the most immediate and ephemeral are assumed to have lives of their own. The broadest contextual elements Fernand Braudel defines simply as time and space, which provide the limits, or "enclosures," of duration and geography within which *conjonctures, structures,* and in fact all human history occurs, and he makes very effective use of these concepts in his *Mediterranean and the Mediterranean World in the Age of Philip II.* The claim of the *Annales* school that their methodology and investigations have enriched such traditional types of history as political and diplomatic, which they originally rejected, is undeniable insofar as they have elucidated the circumstances and dynamics that impinge upon these phases of human activity. Ultimately, however, the validity of their explanations depends upon one's acceptance of their view of historical causation.

Discussions of this vital matter are rare in the publications of the *Annales* school, doubtless because of the breadth of their spectrum and their disinterest in events. Insofar as a theory of causation may be associated with the school, it is implied in their great emphasis upon trends, pressures, and forces of all kinds as these are manifest in *conjonctures* and *structures,* rather than the more traditional association of causation with human decision and agency. Human beings are not ignored, of course, since the study of history is by definition the pursuit of knowledge and understanding of men, but the focus shifts from individuals to their context. In fact, the fundamental position is that individuals are shaped and largely controlled by external forces of various types and operating on various levels. This de-emphasis of the individual in favor of the collectivity and the subjection of both to broader economic, social, and psychological forces with their own dynamics is readily admitted by the leaders of the school. Concerning outstanding and influential figures in the past, Lucien Febvre wrote in his *Combats pour l'histoire:* "The historical individual . . . , or more exactly the historic personage develops in and through the group. He disengages himself from it for a moment and indicates new paths for it. But to accomplish his work . . . he must reenter it as soon as possible, reintegrating himself in the group."[3] Fernand Braudel went considerably further. In terminating his massive *Mediterranean and the Mediterranean World in the Age of Philip II,* he argues that the great king's death had no effect upon the established trends of Spanish history, either at home or abroad. The freedom of the indi-

3. P. 82.

vidual, Braudel claims, is in fact subject to the sharpest limits and is meaningful only if he recognizes these restraints, chooses to remain within them, and exerts himself within their confines. And Braudel concludes: "So when I think of the individual, I am always inclined to see him imprisoned within a destiny in which he himself has little hand, fixed in a landscape in which the infinite perspectives of the long term stretch into the distance both behind him and before. In historical analysis as I see it, rightly or wrongly, the long run always wins in the end."[4] Such a position seems to be the essence of determinism.

This denial of substantial influence to even the most outstanding historical figures may be illustrated by examining the *Annales* school's treatment of Colbert. Because of their great concern for economic *conjonctures*, several members of the school have carefully evaluated Colbert's role in shaping the French economy during the first two decades of Louis XIV's personal reign. In the *Annales* for 1933, Lucien Febvre severely criticized Boissonnade's *Colbert, le triomphe de l'étatisme*, calling it merely a hymn to Colbert and wrongly conceived because it failed to measure his work in the larger context of the French economy. And the current *Annales* school has maintained this position. Representative statements may be found in Jean Meuvret's collected essays, Pierre Deyon's brief but authoritative *Mercantilisme*, Pierre Goubert's *Louis XIV and Twenty Million Frenchmen* and his contributions to the second volume of Labrousse *et al.*, *Histoire économique et sociale de la France*, and Robert Mandrou's *La France aux XVIIe et XVIIIe siècles* and his *Louis XIV en son temps*. All agree that Colbert, far from being the "revolutionary" that Lavisse depicted, was quite unoriginal in his economic theories and was merely a loyal, hardworking agent of the crown who attempted much under very adverse circumstances. In retrospect, his most apparent successes lay in his support of certain industries, his building a navy and merchant marine, his ordinances for commercial affairs, and his lessening of administrative abuses. But these left untouched the economy as a whole and were more than counterbalanced by his mistakes (overregulation of industry and raising indirect taxes) and the failure of his trading companies

4. Vol. II, p. 1244.

and tariff system. The Dutch War, which he favored, was disastrous to his projects, while the inelasticity of French industry
and, above all, the prevailing chronic deflation (usually called
Phase B according to Simiand's categories, in contradistinction
to the inflationary Phase A, which ended about 1630) completely defeated his efforts. Goubert and Mandrou maintain
that Colbert wore himself out attempting misguided projects
in an impossible situation— misguided because they never
touched the foundations of state finances or the general economy and impossible because only the English and Dutch possessed commercial systems that were capable of resisting the
adverse economic currents of the age. All this reduces Colbert's
personal achievements to minuscule proportions indeed. And
Jean Delumeau, in a special issue of *XVII* *Siècle* (1966) on the
French economy in the seventeenth century, goes so far as to
state that the gains that were registered during Colbert's ministry would have occurred without him because they resulted
from established trends in the economy and the absence of
major internal strife after the failure of the Fronde. Conditions,
not men, were decisive.

And what of Louis XIV? An examination of the *Annales*
school's treatment of his place in history should provide a valuable index to their determinism, since there is no denying his
personal importance in his own time. Fortunately, we have two
books by leaders of the school who address themselves to this
issue: Goubert's *Louis XIV and Twenty Million Frenchmen* and
Mandrou's *Louis XIV en son temps*. The major difference between these books is one of scope, since Goubert focuses upon
France whereas Mandrou examines western Europe generally,
but otherwise they have much in common. The objective of
both authors is to place Louis XIV in the context of his time
and to measure his achievements and significance accordingly.
In doing this, they depart from the method used by Braudel
in his *Mediterranean and the Mediterranean World in the Age
of Philip II*, since it is generally conceded that when Braudel
devoted the first two-thirds of his work to the inumerable elements, *structures*, and *conjonctures* of life in the Mediterranean
area and then added an account of political developments during Philip II's reign—the portion of the book that he found

least significant and interesting—he failed to present an integrated picture of Philip II in his time. Goubert and Mandrou, on the contrary, examine the relevance of Louis XIV's policies throughout many portions of their works, but the extent to which they succeed in determining his exact historical import remains to be seen.

In structuring their treatments of Louis XIV's reign, Goubert and Mandrou take into account much recent research on economic and social matters, the main concerns of the *Annales* school. Major portions of this research, however, are either very fragmentary or as yet incomplete, as both authors recognize, and their books are therefore intended more as interim reports than definitive presentations. The result is that both incorporate into their narratives much traditionally accepted information, often uncritically, merely placing it in a new framework. And since the relationships between these two elements are not always clear, this hinders their efforts to place the king adequately in the context of his times. It also causes them frequently to revert to the positions that were utilized by earlier historians, particularly Lavisse. Thus the two books, while the best that we have from the *Annales* school, are not their last word on the subject.

When assessing the all-important matter of Louis XIV's motivation and objectives, Goubert and Mandrou make extensive use of the king's view of himself and his understanding of divine-right absolutism that are set forth in his memoirs. And both conclude that his great desire for personal glory and domination was the primary motive force behind many if not most of his policies. The position is obviously reminiscent of Lavisse, who built his work on essentially the same foundation. Goubert and Mandrou find Louis XIV's thirst for personal glory and dominion over all, both at home and abroad, to have been constant throughout his reign, and they consequently measure his achievements against this impossibly lofty ideal, inevitably finding that he generally failed to achieve his objectives. The approach is simplistic for several reasons. It ignores the unreliable nature of Louis XIV's memoirs as guides to his motivation throughout his entire reign. There were obviously many modifications of his attitudes and objectives in the course of his very long reign, as historians have long recognized, but these are glossed over in both volumes. Also, their great emphasis upon the king's desire for domination causes both authors to present him in a position of almost constant confrontation with all other parties, both his French subjects and the other nations of western Europe. There is much truth in this position, but again important modifications are necessary, particularly in works that attempt to place Louis XIV in the context of his time. Louis XIV's relations with other individuals, groups, and nations often involved as much participation as confrontation, especially in domestic affairs and even in foreign affairs during the latter portion of the reign. In addition, this emphasis on confrontation and domination often causes both authors to move from the power center outward when treating internal matters rather than the opposite, which is more characteristic of recent economic and social analysis. Again the position is reminiscent of Lavisse.

True to the traditions of the *Annales* school, Goubert and Mandrou open their discussions of France under Louis XIV by sketching its economic and social foundations. The impression that they convey is one of extreme fragmentation in all categories, although they show that French society was fundamentally strong and was held together and made functional by an equilibrium of forces and various continuing *structures*. Having made this important point, they then take up the efforts of Louis XIV and his aides to establish direct controls over all elements of the population. This objective was pursued throughout the reign, they contend, but the greatest successes were achieved in the first two decades of Louis XIV's personal rule. Although the intendants encountered varying types and degrees of resistance, they generally succeeded in establishing royal domination over all segments of French society. The great nobles were domesticated; the Parlements and provincial estates were brought to heel; the Church and such dissident groups as the Jansenists and Huguenots felt the weight of royal oppression; the guilds saw their traditional liberties infringed; and the military effectively neutralized peasant uprisings. All this, of course, is to be found in such traditional works as Lavisse and is here presented with surprisingly few changes. Man-

drou extends his analysis of increased royal controls to what
he calls the mobilization and direction of all the arts and letters
"simply and solely for the glory of the monarch."[5] Here he points
to such well-known items as the work of the academies, the
censorship, the building of Versailles, and the prohibition of
teaching of Cartesian philosophy. Regarding Louis XIV's religious policies, Mandrou finds the climax of Gallicanism in the
famous Four Articles of 1682 to be mere extension of royal
control over the Church, but he enters a new note regarding the
persecution of the Jansenists and Huguenots. Instead of attrib-
uting this to royal and ecclesiastical hatred of religious disunity,
Mandrou would ascribe it to official concern for the great dis-
parity between the primitive, superstitious faith of the masses
and the much more orthodox and sophisticated beliefs of the
elite. In other words, he introduces the broader context of
popular culture as a major factor in determining official policy.
Although the argument is not entirely convincing, it is one of
the few new views in this portion of both works.

Somewhat more novel is their treatment of Louis XIV's
early wars, the War of Devolution and the Dutch War. Both
are shown to have been motivated chiefly by the king's desire
for increased personal glory and domination of Europe in a
uniquely favorable situation. The major obstacle to French
hegemony was the Dutch, whom Louis XIV despised and Colbert hated as France's natural enemy. Both believed that France
could reduce this minuscule nation to the status of a fifth-rate
state, but in this they were wrong, Goubert and Mandrou insist,
because conditions had drastically changed in favor of the
maritime powers and this was realized by neither Louis XIV nor
Colbert. Thus, while the Sun King hailed the outcome of the
Dutch War as a great victory because of his territorial gains,
it was in reality a disaster. Goubert interprets the war almost
exclusively in economic terms, showing how it brought to an
abrupt end any successes that Colbert may have achieved in
the years of peace. Mandrou gives a broader interpretation of
the war, representing it as a clash of two very different civilizations. In describing all that the Dutch stood for, Mandrou
dwells extensively upon their great prosperity, the success

5. P. 159.

of their industrial, commercial, and banking systems, their achievements in intellectual and artistic endeavors, their religious toleration, and, above all, their regime of personal liberty. It was these qualities that gave resilience to the Dutch system, says Mandrou, expressing great admiration for the little nation that successfully resisted the onslaught of the most powerful military machine in Europe. While ostensibly the victor, Louis XIV was in reality defeated by forces beyond his control and even his comprehension.

The dramatic 1680s, when Louis XIV was at the height of his power and most aggressive, are described by Goubert and Mandrou simply as the climax of his perennial policy of glory and domination both at home and abroad. Although the nation's economy, as Goubert details, was suffering from chronic deflation, bad harvests, and the burdens of war, Louis XIV relentlessly pursued his policy of force and self-glorification. Religious despotism (both authors use the term) reached its climax in the struggle with the papacy and the revocation of the Edict of Nantes. In foreign affairs, Louvois may have had some influence, but it was the king who determined policy. His aggressions were permitted to him, Mandrou points out, merely by the undeniable superiority of the French military establishment and troubles in many other realms. The reunions were mere legal chicanery backed by force in a momentarily favorable situation. Other acts of aggression were equally unjustified. The Truce of Ratisbon (1684) merely gave sanction to a policy of brutality which was bound to fail because it was made possible only by temporary conditions and was therefore anachronistic.

The period of decline (ca. 1685–1715)—for both authors see it thus—is described in the most somber terms. At the extreme pinnacle, the aging monarch lacked capable ministers while blindly pursuing his established policies. The bureaucracy greatly expanded but with lesser men in charge, and was faced with insurmountable problems. The wars of the period, which were initiated without regard for their consequences and under intrinsically adverse conditions, were the major cause of decline. The financial situation of the state soon became desperate and forced the revival of all questionable measures. The impact upon French society increased in severity as one descended the social scale: the financiers thrived while the privileged classes and the robe were little affected, but exploitation, misery, famine, disease, and the forcible levying of troops were the lot of the masses. The net decline in population, caused partially by decreased births and extensive emigration, was dramatic. The general economy could not but suffer. Foreign trade fell sharply, although it rebounded during the War of the Spanish Succession, as did certain wartime industries, creating pockets of prosperity in a generally adverse situation. Most fundamental, these factors plus continuing deflation punctuated by bad harvests and sharply fluctuating grain prices forced a sharp decline of agriculture, the basis of the national economy. The resources of the state fell accordingly because of the decline of the population and the number of taxables.

Meanwhile, Mandrou shows, France was rapidly losing ground even in her vaunted cultural and intellectual activity. Versailles declined as a center of cultural life both because of its new, somber tone and its failure to attract new talent. What intellectual life there was moved to Paris and provincial centers, where new schools and academies were founded and canons of taste evolved away from the classical and grandiose toward the natural and intimate. Even more important was the patent failure of Louis XIV's religious policies. Arch-Gallicanism was gradually abandoned in negotiations with the papacy; the Huguenots survived in many areas despite the harshest measures (which Mandrou deplores); and the persecution of the Jansenists caused a massive reaction in the realm of opinion. Religious unity remained as elusive as ever, and in this area Louis XIV's failure was total. Simultaneously, England was forging ahead on all fronts. In international economics, she was rapidly moving into first place with her excellent commercial, imperial, and banking systems. The great flexibility and stability of English society were such that she easily weathered the Glorious Revolution and achieved further political strength. Her cultural life was correspondingly vigorous, with architectural advances in London, the revival of university life, the work of Newton and the Royal Academy, and political writers such as John Locke. All this and much more Mandrou presents in detail, making no attempt to hide his greater admiration for developments on the British side of the Channel.

Regarding the two great wars of the period, both authors see them as merely the fruit of misguided royal policy, although the two conflicts were essentially different. Goubert contents himself with showing that in the War of the League of Augsburg Louis XIV completely failed to achieve any of the objectives that he set for himself in 1689. Mandrou points to Louis XIV's disastrous loss of allies which resulted from offensive diplomacy and acts of violence, and finds the war inconclusive except to strengthen England and the Emperor for the next round. The War of the Spanish Succession, of course, presented special problems, but again both authors recount French diplomacy in an unfavorable manner. After giving scant attention to the partition treaties, both represent Louis XIV's acceptance of Carlos II's will as motivated by relatively narrow personal and dynastic motives and a willingness to defy almost all Europe. And very interestingly, both greatly emphasize the economic implications of the war even while admitting that these were the least of Louis XIV's calculations. Goubert argues that the union of France with Spain and her empire made excellent economic sense and brought momentary advantages, and Mandrou agrees, adding that the allies were fully aware of the economic issue and determined to turn it to their advantage. In other words, Louis XIV entered the war for misguided personal reasons and neglected the economic, which was ultimately the most significant. This was signalized by the Peace of Utrecht, in which the British gained economic preponderance and a new balance of power was established. Mandrou concludes that despite heroic eleventh-hour actions on the part of the French and their avoidance of greater disaster, Utrecht marked the defeat of all that Louis XIV's absolutism stood for. Not only did he fail to achieve his objectives of 1700–1702; he was defeated by a nation with a superior system of government and enterprise which was more adapted to the times and gained ascendancy in world affairs. Although few realized it, a new era was dawning which would witness the supremacy of peoples rather than governments. Thus the transfer of preponderance to the British was partially caused by Louis XIV's mistaken policies but more importantly by the superiority of their commercial and governmental systems, which he did not understand and were quite beyond his control.

In concluding their books, both Goubert and Mandrou examine the condition of France when Louis XIV finally died in 1715. Their purpose is to ask whether their new perspectives in any way alter the picture of a France bled white by the Sun King's incessant wars. Both admit the obvious: the massive suffering and exploitation of the lower classes, the sheer decline in population, fiscal chaos in government finance, continuing trouble with the Huguenots, and strife over the bull *Unigenitus*. But Goubert suggests partial revisions of this traditional view, chiefly in the economic sphere. He argues that the contraction of the population was not necessarily a bad thing, since there were fewer mouths to feed and the victims were chiefly the very old and very young, the least productive members of society. Good harvests beginning in 1714 brought lower agricultural prices, and contracts with tenant farmers were reasonable. And the rapid revival of commerce brought new wealth and aided industry. Admittedly, these phenomena were very unevenly scattered throughout the realm, and major islands of prosperity alternated with areas of continuing poverty. Much additional research is needed, Goubert insists, before any extensive, adequately grounded revisionism is attempted, but he believes that additional findings concerning the economic, social, and psychological currents of the period will enable historians to develop a very different picture of the "age of Louis XIV."

For the present, provisional estimates of Louis XIV in his time, as seen by our two leaders of the *Annales* school, are set forth in the conclusions of their two volumes. Goubert aptly remarks that Louis XIV's clearest success was his perpetuation of the legend of his greatness, but Goubert also believes that the Sun King's renown is quite undeserved. He expanded the realm only to lose most of his conquests before his death. His effort for religious uniformity was a total failure. His patronage of arts and letters succeeded for fifteen years but rapidly dwindled as governmental expenses multiplied and tastes and intellectual currents moved away from him. His intendants were strengthened, but their dominance over all elements of the population encountered massive resistance and was a source of future trouble. His new codes of law were brilliantly conceived but indifferently applied. His diplomats were the ablest in Europe but were opposed by those of England and the United Provinces, which possessed superior economic and governmental systems. Louvois's standing army was a major achievement but was hated and feared by the populace. Colbert's navy was strong at first, then declined. Colbert accomplished much during the early, peaceful years of the reign, but his projects were ruined by war and he completely failed to reform state finances or the general economy.

The root causes of these many failures both Goubert and Mandrou find not in Louis XIV's lack of determination but in the irresistible, adverse forces that determined conditions of life both in France and in Europe at large. French society, although fragmented and riddled with frictions, was essentially sound and Louis XIV's efforts to dominate and exploit it inevitably ran afoul of intense localism and hostility to controls of any kind. Even more important were the chronic economic depression and monetary famine (Phase B), which reduced the resources of the state and undercut many of the Sun King's enterprises. Only the British and Dutch successfully withstood these challenges, with the result that economic dominance moved to England and bypassed France with her rigid controls and static economy. As for the cultural significance of the reign, both authors recognize the greatness of classical culture at its height but stress its rapid decline because of changes in ideas and taste. The beginnings of the Enlightenment and the rise of the rococo soon negated all that Versailles stood for. Thus Louis XIV was confronted with insuperable *conjonctures* on the all-important social, economic, and cultural counts. Mandrou concludes that the Sun King's policies—sitting as he did in Versailles, isolated in the midst of great pomp, surrounded with medals struck in his honor, and as avid for glory and domination as ever—were thoroughly anachronistic because impossible, and impossible because they ran counter to the basic currents of his time. Thus the reign was essentially a failure because the king's ideals and objectives could not be applied in practice. His few achievements did not justify their great cost. And Mandrou even refers approvingly to Michelet, who condemned the reign as an era of tyranny, violence, persecution, and misery, all because of Louis XIV's enormous pride. It would seem that Mandrou's work, the most recent estimate of the Sun King from the *Annales* school, comes close to writing off his reign as a dead end.

This, of course, is far from the last word on the subject from the *Annales* school, since both Mandrou and Goubert intend their books to be provisional reports rather than definitive analyses. Their defects, however, should not pass unnoticed. The fundamental question to ask in concluding this survey is whether these works contribute substantially to our understanding of Louis XIV. The objective of both authors to present Louis XIV in the broader context of his own time is laudable and indeed indispensable, but there are serious weaknesses in its execution. The economic and social contexts are masterly in their presentation, as far as present knowledge permits, although the psychological is much less developed, again reflecting the current state of knowledge. But after analyzing the setting, both examine royal policy largely from the standpoint of its impact on all and sundry, both at home and abroad. This creates a fundamental dichotomy between the ruler and the major currents of his time and causes both authors to present Louis XIV almost as an extraneous element in his age rather than a part of it. Louis XIV may have been moving against the tide of history in certain fundamental ways, as later developments would demonstrate, but in his own day he also brought to fruition much that had been growing under monarchical leadership for centuries. Thus it is hardly adequate to maintain that his basic position was one of confrontation with his own world.

In addition, in their narratives both Goubert and Mandrou present much conventional material, often uncritically. Political history necessarily bulks large in the reign of Louis XIV, and innumerable events were obviously crucial to the fortunes of king and nation alike. But the bias of the *Annales* school against *histoire événementielle* doubtless caused both authors to give minimum attention to the specifics in their narratives. The result is that they simply fit much traditional information into the broader framework without adequately checking its details. Ragnhild Hatton has had no trouble identifying errors in Goubert's account of Louis XIV's diplomacy, and inaccuracies in other areas might be cited. Clearly there is need for a more painstaking analysis of the many elements of Louis XIV's policies and their precise relationships with the innumerable facets of the period.

Most disappointing is their treatment of Louis XIV. As a humanistic study, history is an attempt to understand human beings in all their manifold complexities. However, little attempt is made in either book to develop the character of Louis XIV and to present him as a personality. The approach of the school through trends, statistics, and blanket categories seems to have caused both authors to be satisfied with depicting Louis XIV merely as a type. This is especially noticeable in their extremely simplistic exposition of his understanding of absolutism. Relying chiefly upon his memoirs and secondarily upon such trappings of grandeur as medals, portraits, Versailles, and so on, both interpret divine-right absolutism as merely an insatiable lust for personal glory and domination over all others. And to this end they show the Sun King deliberately resorting to violence of all types and descriptions, in both domestic and foreign policy. That the concepts of absolutism and kingly grandeur were much more complex has long been known. Furthermore, neither author finds Louis XIV varying significantly from his archetypal position throughout his entire reign. Although the core of his principles remained intact, both his attitude and his methods changed with circumstances, and the later Louis XIV was in many respects quite different from the earlier. Again a much more painstaking analysis of his conduct, objectives, and underlying motives in each period of the reign is needed for historical accuracy.

All this means that the measurements that are used in both volumes are faulty or at least arbitrary. Louis XIV's achievements are assessed by contrasting his static, absolutistic objectives with his actual gains. Inevitably, both authors find that he repeatedly failed because he was checkmated by the broader currents of his time. Thus the king was out of joint with his age and his efforts were anachronistic. This was doubtless true during certain portions of his reign, but there were others when Louis XIV's equation of his personal glory with the interests of the nation made excellent sense to his contemporaries. The charge that his policies were anachronistic essentially means that he failed to understand that he was living in deflationary Phase B and did not realize that the British and Dutch systems were the wave of the future. The accusation is unhistorical in that it is based on a knowledge of later developments which were quite unknown in his time.

It should be clear from this survey that the *Annales* school, far from seeking answers to traditional questions, is posing new ones based on different perspectives and methodologies. And this in turn has caused certain divergences between French historical scholarship and much of the work of British and American historians. Instead of searching for answers to such traditional questions as the relations between Louis XIV and his ministers, the functioning of diplomacy and institutions, the uniqueness of each period of the reign, and the issue of its essential greatness, the *Annales* school has chosen to emphasize contextual factors on the assumption that they largely determine human activity. In doing so, they have developed much information that was unknown to Louis XIV and his contemporaries, and have added extensively to our knowledge of the period. But their treatment of great and influential individuals leaves much to be desired. In the process of contextual analysis, the leaders of the school have produced a determinism in which Louis XIV, the most consequential personality in Europe, is little more than a proponent of principles that were opposed to the stream of history and bound to fail. The position is patently too rigid and needs much modification and refinement. But these are weaknesses that may be expected from interim reports. As the perennial search for historical truth unfolds, it is reasonable to hope for more sophisticated interpretations of Louis XIV's reign from the members of the *Annales* school.

4. Conclusion

At the present time, no single historian or school of thought predominates in the historiography of Louis XIV. So rich is the subject that new perspectives are constantly being developed and knowledge is continually expanding—a normal and healthy state of affairs in the investigation of any memorable period. Of the many historians whose contributions we have analyzed, however, three may be singled out for special mention. The two basic, generic positions are those of Voltaire, who viewed the "age of Louis XIV" as great because of the cultural climax that it embodied, and Lemontey, who first gave extensive attention to Louis XIV's development of the administrative state and the rapid decline of the monarchy's national foundations late in his reign. And almost a century after Lemontey, Ernest Lavisse produced his memorable synthesis, which in many respects has never been superseded. Major portions of his brilliant analysis of Louis XIV's reign retain great value, both for their content and as points of departure for further investigations. His views concerning Colbert's "offer" to Louis XIV of an economically sound France and the nature of French foreign policy have been extensively rectified, but important elements of his treatment of internal affairs reappear in the most recent treatises, as we have noted. And despite its sweeping nature, his claim that Louis XIV brought absolute monarchy to perfection but rendered it incapable of further development, thus sealing its doom, has not been convincingly challenged. Although recent studies have emphasized the decentralization of controls in the eighteenth century and the adaptation of the monarchy to changing conditions, the fact remains that Louis XIV established the final form of monarchical government in France before the Revolution.

Regarding Louis XIV as a personality and as king, much is known, but there remain ample areas for further study. A genuine consensus, however, has long decreed his vital significance to the fortunes of France and Europe in his own time. Even those like Michelet who generally condemn his policies and others such as Goubert and Mandrou who find them anachronistic are indirectly paying tribute to his great stature and momentous impact in his age. The unanswered questions concerning the king have chiefly to do with his personal qualities, ideals, and motivation. These matters have also been extensively examined, but their more subtle elements have resisted analysis. It is not enough to repeat such terms as "egotism," "glory," "grandeur," and "domination" when describing Louis XIV's personal values and understanding of his mission as divinely appointed absolute ruler of the greatest nation in Europe. It is necessary to appreciate how he *felt* these things and how they guided his conduct. Further cognizance of these vital components of his life would extensively elucidate his relations with his ministers and his determination of policy, especially in foreign affairs. Also, these elements of his being patently evolved throughout his long reign, and it is necessary to examine the alterations in his personality and ideals in many consecutive periods. The entire matter is extremely difficult because of its great subtlety and many imponderables, which are unsusceptible of finite measurement and must, in the final analysis, be handled in a subjective, impressionistic way. Fortunately, Louis XIV's personal qualities and their evolution are currently under investigation, not from the psychoanalytic standpoint but as they were manifest in his actions during different portions of his reign. The resulting studies should go far to indicate the extent to which he subsumed the values of the French nation in this moment of greatness.

Knowledge of the various elements of Louis XIV's government similarly reflects both mature scholarship and many unknowns which are the subjects of current research. Despite great earlier advances, the three decades since World War II have witnessed major contributions by American and British scholars, and the *Annales* school has opened up whole new vistas, bringing exciting new developments in many areas. Economic currents have been subjected to new scrutiny, incidentally revising estimates of Colbert. Louis XIV's much vaunted control over all elements of French society has been reexamined in the light of a new understanding of social dynamics. The all important institutional aspects of Louis XIV's state-building are being investigated, especially in the last generation of the reign, while Mousnier's reorientation of institutional history places the growth of the administrative state in a new framework. Much is known concerning Louis XIV's religious policies, but questions are being asked concerning the influence of religious considerations upon his decisions in other areas. Regarding Louis XIV's foreign policy and wars, which have been debated for centuries, there is still no consensus concerning the precise extent to which they were motivated by his great desire for glory and domination, the exact place of each episode—for example, the Dutch War—within his larger objectives, and the degree to which his actions ran counter to contemporary values, as in the 1680s, which many analysts decry as the nadir of his foreign policy. All these matters are under examination, period by period, especially as they relate to the final generation of the reign. As for the adverse impact of Louis XIV's policies during his last thirty years, the once gloomy picture is being modified by examination of his relatively statesmanlike diplomacy, his newly enlightened understanding of national interests, the persistence of many foci of prosperity, and the rapid recovery of the French economy after the Peace of Utrecht. But whether such findings will neutralize the criticisms of Louis XIV's contemporaries, Lemontey's dictum that the monarchy rapidly lost its roots in the nation, and the widely accepted idea that Louis XIV lived too long for his reputation remains to be seen.

Finally, was the greatness of the "age of Louis XIV" due in large measure to the work of the king? An accident of chronology places the two proponents of seemingly opposite views — Voltaire and the *Annales* school—at the extreme ends of our time span, yet their differences are more apparent than real.

Voltaire, writing from a frankly elitist viewpoint, depicted Louis XIV's many contributions to the life of the nation and the triumph of French classical culture under his aegis, whereas Goubert and Mandrou maintain that his efforts in all areas were opposed by strong contemporary currents and were largely abortive in the long run. But the latter position does not negate the lasting achievements of French letters or the significance of Louis XIV's patronage of many fields in his own time. Neither does the *Annales* school's emphasis on popular culture, which seems singularly inappropriate in this context. Thus Voltaire's position, essentially continued by Lavisse, remains valid, and the period in fact witnessed a genuine cultural climax. And on the much broader stage of Europe at large, the reality of French leadership and hegemony is undeniable. Louis XIV's errors of policy and misuse of power notwithstanding, he contributed as much to the growth of Europe as the leader of any other nation during its moment of preeminence. His reign served as a catalyst, both in France and abroad, for the development of the nation-state, the principal framework of modern European life. And he did so while incomparably fulfilling the political ideology of his time, divine-right absolutism. Thus Louis XIV stands as the fitting sovereign of France, symbolic of all that she represented, during the last great age of her monarchy.

Bibliography

This bibliography lists only the items that are referred to in this book, plus a few others that are illustrative of the trends discussed.

The **boldface** numbers following entries indicate pages on which the author or the work is mentioned in the text.

* Books in paperback edition are marked with an asterisk.

*Acton, Lord. *Lectures on Modern History*. London, 1956.   **46**

Adam, A. *Du Mysticisme à la révolte: Les Jansénistes du XVIIe siècle*. Paris, 1968.   **83**

Aiglun, Rochas d', ed. *Vauban, sa famille et ses écrits, ses oisivetés et sa correspondance*. 2 vols. Paris, 1910.   **45**

André, L. *Louis XIV et l'Europe*. Paris, 1950.   **85**

————. *Michel Le Tellier et l'organisation de l'armée monarchique*. Paris, 1906.   **43**

————. *Michel Le Tellier et Louvois*. Paris, 1942.   **63**

Antoine, M. *Le Conseil du roi sous le règne de Louis XV*. Geneva, 1970.   **76**

Asher, E. L. *The Resistance to the Maritime Classes: The Survival of Feudalism in the France of Colbert*. Berkeley, 1960.   **79**

"Aspects de l'économie française au XVIIe siècle," in *XVIIe Siècle*, Nos. 70–71 (1966).

Aumale, Duc d'. *Histoire des princes de Condé, pendant les XVIe et XVIIe siècles*. 8 vols. Paris, 1863–96.   **39**

Avrigny, H. d'. *Mémoires chronologiques pour servir à l'histoire universelle de l'Europe depuis 1600 jusqu'en 1716*. 4 vols. Paris, 1720.   **15**

Bailly, A. *Le Règne de Louis XIV*. Paris, 1946.   **68**

Baird, H. M. *The Huguenots and the Revocation of the Edict of Nantes*. 2 vols. New York, 1895.   **44**

Baudrillart, A. *Philippe V et la cour de France*. 5 vols. Paris, 1890–1901.   **43**

Baxter, S. B. *William III*. London, 1966.   **88**

Bernard, L. *The Emerging City: Paris in the Age of Louis XIV*. Durham, N.C., 1970.   **69**

————. "French Society and Popular Uprisings under Louis XIV," *French Historical Studies*, III (1964), 454–74.   **81**

Blet, P. *Le Clergé de France et la monarchie*, Vol. II: *1645–1666*. Rome, 1959.   **82**

Bloch, M. *Les Rois thaumaturges*. Strasbourg, 1924.   **60**

————. *The Royal Touch: Sacred Monarchy and Scrofula in England and France*. English translation. London, 1973.

Boisguillebert. *Détail de la France; Factum de la France*, E. Daire, ed. Paris, 1843.   **45**

Boislisle, A. de, ed. *Correspondance des controleurs généraux des finances avec les intendants des provinces, 1683–1715*. 3 vols. Paris, 1874–97.   **42**

————, ed. *Mémoires de Saint-Simon*. 43 vols. Paris, 1879–1930.   **39**

————, ed. *Mémoires des intendants sur l'état des généralités dressés pour l'instruction du Duc de Bourgogne*. Paris, 1881.   **41**

Boislisle, J. de, ed. *Mémoriaux du conseil de 1661.* 3 vols. Paris, 1905–7.
42
Boissonnade, P. *Colbert, le triomphe de l'étatisme, la fondation de la su-prématie industrielle de la France, la dictature du travail (1661–1683).* Paris, 1932.   61, 78, 98
Bossuet. *Discours sur l'histoire universelle.* Paris, 1681.   15
Boulenger, J. *Le Grand Siècle.* Paris, 1911.   46
———. *The Seventeenth Century.* English translation. New York, 1920.
Bourgeois, E. *Le Grand Siècle.* Paris, 1896.   40
———. *France under Louis XIV.* English translation. New York, 1897.
Braubach, M. *Versailles und Wien von Ludwig XIV bis Kaunitz.* Bonn, 1952.   85
Braudel, F. *Écrits sur l'histoire.* Paris, 1969.
———. *La Méditerranée et le monde méditerranéen à l'époque de Philippe II.* Paris, 1949, 1966.   97, 99
*———. *The Mediterranean and the Mediterranean World in the Age of Philip II.* 2 vols., English translation. New York, 1972.
———. "Personal Testimony," *Journal of Modern History,* XLIV (1972), 448–67.
Cadet, F. *Pierre de Boisguillebert, précurseur des économistes, 1646–1714: Sa Vie, ses travaux, son influence.* Paris, 1870.   45
Carré, H. *L'Enfance et la première jeunesse de Louis XIV, 1638–1661.* Paris, 1944.   68
———. *The Early Life of Louis XIV (1638–1661).* English translation. London, 1951.
Champigneulles, B., ed. *Louis XIV: Mémoires et divers écrits.* Paris, 1960.   70
Chaunu, P. "Les Crises au XVIIᵉ siècle de l'Europe réformée," *Revue his-torique,* CCXXX (1965), 23–60.   84
Chérot, H. *La Première Jeunesse de Louis XIV.* Lille, 1892.   39
Chéruel, A. *Histoire de France pendant la minorité de Louis XIV.* 4 vols. Paris, 1879–80.   39
———. *Histoire de France sous le ministère de Mazarin (1651–1661).* 3 vols. Paris, 1882.   39
———, ed. *Lettres du Cardinal Mazarin pendant son ministère.* 6 vols. Paris, 1872–90.   39
Clément, P., ed. *Lettres, instructions et mémoires de Colbert.* 7 vols. Paris, 1861–73.   41
———. *Histoire de la vie et l'administration de Colbert.* Paris, 1846.   41
———. *Le Gouvernement de Louis XIV, ou la cour, l'administration, les finances et le commerce de 1683 à 1689.* Paris, 1848.   41
———. *Madame de Montespan et Louis XIV.* Paris, 1868.   40
———. *La Police sous Louis XIV.* Paris, 1866.   41
Cognet, L. *Le Jansénisme.* Paris, 1968.   83
Cole, C. W. *Colbert and a Century of French Mercantilism.* 2 vols. New York, 1939.   62, 78
"Comment les français voyaient la France au XVIIᵉ siècle," in *XVIIᵉ Siècle,* Nos. 25–26 (1955).
Cordelier, J. *Madame de Maintenon.* Paris, 1955.   69
Cronin, V. *Louis XIV.* Boston, 1965.   68
Dangeau, Marquis de. *Journal de la cour de Louis XIV,* Soulié *et al.,* eds. 19 vols. Paris, 1854–60.   39, 45
Daniel, G. *Histoire de France depuis l'établissement de la monarchie française dans les Gaules.* 3 vols. Paris, 1713.   14

Dent, J. *Crisis in Finance: Crown, Financiers and Society in Seventeenth-Century France.* New York, 1973.   74

Depping, G., ed. *Correspondance administrative sous le règne de Louis XIV.* 4 vols. Paris, 1850–55.   42

Deyon, P. *Le Mercantilisme.* Paris, 1969.   98

Dreyss, C., ed. *Mémoires de Louis XIV pour l'instruction du dauphin.* 2 vols. Paris, 1860.   40, 60

Droz, J. *Histoire diplomatique de 1648 à 1919.* Paris, 1952.   85, 86

Druon, H. *Histoire de l'éducation des princes dans la maison des Bourbons de France.* 2 vols. Paris, 1897.   39

Dumont, F. "Royauté française et monarchie absolue au XVIIe siècle," *XVIIe Siècle,* Nos. 58–59 (1963), 3–29.   71

Erlanger, P. *Louis XIV.* Paris, 1966.

———. *Louis XIV,* English translation. New York, 1970.

Esmonin, E. *Études sur la France des XVIIe et XVIIIe siècles* [collected essays]. Paris, 1964.   64

Farmer, J. E. *Versailles and the Court under Louis XIV.* New York, 1905.   40

Faugère, A. P., ed. *Écrits inédits de Saint-Simon.* 8 vols. Paris, 1880–93.   45

Febvre, L. *Combats pour l'histoire.* Paris, 1953, 1965.   97

———. *Pour Une Histoire à part entière.* Paris, 1962.

"Fénelon et le tricentenaire de sa naissance, 1651–1951," in *XVIIe Siècle,* Nos. 12, 13, 14 (1952).   93

Fox, P. W. "Louis XIV and the Theories of Absolutism and Divine Right," *Canadian Journal of Economics and Political Science,* XXVI (1960), 128–42.   71, 72

La France au temps de Louis XIV [essays by G. Mongrédien, J. Meuvret, R. Mousnier, R.-A. Weigert, R. Mandrou, A. Adam, V.-L. Tapié]. Paris, 1965.   87

Fréville, H. *L'Intendance de Bretagne (1689–1790),* Vol. 1. Paris, 1953.   76

Furet, F. "Quantitative History," *Daedalus* (Winter, 1971), 151–67, and *Historical Studies Today,* F. Gilbert and S. R. Graubard, eds. New York, 1972.

Gallouédec-Genuys, F. *Le Prince selon Fénelon.* Paris, 1963.   93

*Garlan, Y., and C. Nières. *Les Révoltes bretonnes de 1675: Papier timbré et bonnets rouges.* Paris, 1975.   81

Gaxotte, P. *La France de Louis XIV.* Paris, 1946.   68

———. *The Age of Louis XIV.* English translation. New York, 1970.

Geffroy, A. *Madame de Maintenon.* 2 vols. Paris, 1887.   40

Gérin, C. *Louis XIV et le Saint-Siège.* 2 vols. Paris, 1894.   44

———. *Recherches historiques sur l'assemblée du clergé de France de 1682.* Paris, 1869.   44

Glasson, E. *Le Parlement de Paris: Son Rôle politique depuis le règne de Charles VII jusqu'à la Révolution.* 2 vols. Paris, 1901.   39

Glénisson, J. "L'Historiographie française contemporaine: Tendances et réalisations," in *La Recherche historique en France de 1940 à 1965.* Paris, 1965.   94

Godard, C. *Les Pouvoirs des intendants sous Louis XIV, particulièrement dans les pays d'élections, de 1661 à 1715.* Paris, 1901.   42

Göhring, M. *Weg und Sieg der modernen Staatsidee in Frankreich.* Tübingen, 1947.   71

Goubert, P. *L'Ancien Régime.* 2 vols. Paris, 1969, 1973.

°———. *The Ancient Regime.* English translation. New York, 1974.
———. "Historical Demography and the Reinterpretation of Early Modern French History: A Research Review," *Journal of Interdisciplinary History,* I (1970–71), 37–48.
———. *Louis XIV et vingt millions de français.* Paris, 1966.   **98, 99**
°———. *Louis XIV and Twenty Million Frenchmen.* English translation. New York, 1966.   **98, 99**
Grassby, R. B. "Social Status and Commercial Enterprise under Louis XIV," *Economic History Review,* 2nd ser., XIII (1960), 19–38.   **79**
Grouvelle, P. A. *Œuvres de Louis XIV.* 6 vols. Paris, 1806.   **22**
Guizot, F. *Histoire générale de la civilisation en Europe.* Paris, 1840.   **30**
Hardré, J., ed. *Letters of Louvois.* Chapel Hill, N.C., 1949.   **78**
Hartung, F. "L'État c'est moi," *Historische Zeitschrift,* CLXIX (1949), 1–30.   **71**
Hartung, F., and R. Mousnier. "Quelques Problèmes concernant la monarchie absolue," *Relazioni del X Congresso Internazionale di Scienze Storiche, Rome, 1955,* Vol. IV, 3–55. Florence, 1955.   **71**
Hastier, L. *Louis XIV et Madame de Maintenon.* Paris, 1957.   **69**
°Hatton, R. M. *Europe in the Age of Louis XIV.* London, 1969.
———. *Louis XIV and His World.* New York, 1972.   **90**
———. "Louis XIV: Recent Gains in Historical Knowledge," *Journal of Modern History,* XLV (1973), 277–91.   **90**
Hatton, R. M., and M. S. Anderson, eds. *Studies in Diplomatic History: Essays in Memory of David Bayne Horn.* London, 1970.   **89, 90**
Hatton, R. M., and J. S. Bromley, eds. *Essays 1680–1720 by and for Mark A. Thomson.* Liverpool, 1968.   **88, 89, 90**
Hexter, J. H. "Fernand Braudel and the *Monde Braudellien,*" *Journal of Modern History,* XLIV (1972), 480–539.   **94**
"Histoire métallique" [popular name given to the book *Médailles sur les principaux événements du règne de Louis le Grand,* published by the Académie des Inscriptions et Médailles in 1702].   **14**
Houssaye, A. *Mademoiselle de La Vallière et Madame de Montespan.* Paris, 1860.   **40**
Janet, P. *Fénelon.* Paris, 1892.   **45**
Kantorowicz, E. H. *The King's Two Bodies: A Study in Medieval Political Theology.* Princeton, 1957.   **72**
King, J. E. *Science and Rationalism in the Government of Louis XIV: 1661–1683.* Baltimore, 1949.   **77**
Kossmann, E. H. *La Fronde.* Leiden, 1954.
Krieger, L., and F. Stern, eds. *The Responsibility of Power: Historical Essays in Honor of Hajo Holborn.* New York, 1967.   **88**
Labrousse, E., P. Léon, *et al. Histoire économique et sociale de la France,* Vol. II: *1660–1789.* Paris, 1970.   **98**
Lacour-Gayet, G. *L'Éducation politique de Louis XIV.* Paris, 1898, 1923.   **40**
La Force, Duc de. *Louis XIV et sa cour.* Paris, 1956.   **69**
Lair, J. *Louise de La Vallière et la jeunesse de Louis XIV.* Paris, 1881.   **40**
Langlois, M. *Madame de Maintenon.* Paris, 1932.   **61**
———, ed. *Madame de Maintenon: Lettres,* Vols. 2–5. Paris, 1935–39.   **61**
———. "Madame de Maintenon: Ses Œuvres complètes, la légende et l'histoire," *Revue historique,* CLXVIII (1931), 254–99.   **61**

La Roncière, C. de. *Histoire de la marine française*, Vol. V. Paris, 1919. 62

Larrey, I. de. *Histoire de France sous le règne de Louis XIV*, 9 vols. Rotterdam, 1718. 15

Latreille, A. "Innocent XI, pape 'janséniste,' directeur de conscience de Louis XIV," *Cahiers d'histoire*, I (1956), 9–39. 82

La Vallée, J. de. *Tableau philosophique du règne de Louis XIV, ou Louis XIV jugé par un français libre*. Strasbourg, 1791. 21

Lavallée, T., ed. *Françoise d'Aubigné, Marquise de Maintenon: Correspondance générale*. 2 vols. Paris, 1865–66. 40

Lavisse, E. *Histoire de France*, Vols. 7¹–8¹. Paris, 1911. 47

———. "Dialogues entre Louis XIV et Colbert," *Revue de Paris*, Dec. 15, 1900, 677–96; Jan. 1, 1901, 125–38. 52

Lavisse, E., and A. Rambaud, eds. *Histoire générale, du IVᵉ siècle à nos jours*, Vol. 6. Paris, 1895. 45

Legrelle, A. *La Diplomatie française et la succession d'Espagne*. 4 vols. Paris, 1888–92. 42

———. *Louis XIV et Strasbourg*. Paris, 1884. 42

Lemaitre, J. *Fénelon*. Paris, 1910. 45

Lemoine, J. *De La Vallière à Montespan*. Paris, 1902. 40

Lemontey, P.-E. *Essai sur l'établissement monarchique de Louis XIV*. Paris, 1818. 23

Léonard, E. G. *Histoire générale du protestantisme*, Vol. II: *L'Établissement (1564–1700)*. Paris, 1961. 84

Le Roy Ladurie, E. "Révoltes et contestations rurales en France de 1675 à 1788," *Annales: Economies, sociétés, civilisations*, XXIX (1974), 6–22. 81

Levassor, M. *Histoire du règne de Louis XIII*. 10 vols. Amsterdam, 1700–1711. 14

Lewis, W. H. *Louis XIV: An Informal Portrait*. New York, 1959. 69

Limiers, H. P. de. *Annales de la monarchie française depuis son établissement jusqu'à présent*. 2 vols. Amsterdam, 1724. 15

Livet, C. *L'Intendance d'Alsace sous Louis XIV: 1648–1715*. Paris, 1956. 76

———. "Louis XIV et les provinces conquises," *XVIIᵉ Siècle*, No. 16 (1952), 481–507.

Longnon, J., ed. *Mémoires [de Louis XIV] pour les années 1661 et 1666*. Paris, 1923. 60

———. *A King's Lessons in Statecraft*. English translation. London, 1924.

———. *Mémoires de Louis XIV*. Paris, 1927. 60

Lossky, A. *Louis XIV, William III, and the Baltic Crisis of 1683*. Berkeley, 1954.

———. "The Nature of Political Power according to Louis XIV," in Krieger and Stern, eds., *The Responsibility of Power*. New York, 1967. 88

———. *Louis XIV and the Ascendancy of France*. (In preparation.) 77, 78, 82

Luçay, H. de. *Des Origines du pouvoir ministériel en France: Des Secrétaires d'état sous le règne de Louis XIV*. Paris, 1867. 42

Lüthy, H. *La Banque protestante en France, de la révocation de l'édit de Nantes à la Révolution*, Vol. I: *1685–1730*. Paris, 1959. 92

Madelin, L. *Histoire politique, de 1515 à 1804*, Vol. 4 of G. Hanotaux, ed., *Histoire de la nation française*. Paris, 1924. 56

Mandrou, R. *La France aux XVIIᵉ et XVIIIᵉ siècles*. Paris, 1967. 98

———. *Louis XIV en son temps*. Paris, 1973. 98, 99

———. *Introduction à la France moderne: Essai de psychologie historique, 1500–1640.* Paris, 1961.
———. "L'Historiographie française des XVIe et XVIIe siècles: Bilans et perspectives," *French Historical Studies,* V (1967), 57–66.
Martimort, A.-G. *Le Gallicanisme de Bossuet.* Paris, 1953.   83
———. *Le Gallicanisme.* Paris, 1973.
Martin, H. *Histoire de France,* 4th ed. 17 vols. Paris, 1855–60.   31
Maurois, A. *Louis XIV à Versailles.* Paris, 1955.
*Méthivier, H. *La France de Louis XIV.* Paris, 1975.
Meuvret, J. *Études d'histoire économique.* Paris, 1971.   92, 98
Mézeray, F. E. de. *Abrégé chronologique ou extrait de l'histoire de France.* Paris, 1668, 1672.   14
———. *Histoire de France depuis Pharamond jusqu'à maintenant.* Paris, 1643, 1685.   14
Michaud, E. *Louis XIV et Innocent XI.* 4 vols. Paris, 1882–83.   44
Michel, A. *Louvois et les protestants.* Paris, 1870.   44
Michelet, J. *Histoire de France,* Vols. 13, 14. Paris, 1860, 1862.   34
Mongrédien, G. *Colbert.* Paris, 1963.   78
Moote, A. L. *The Revolt of the Judges: The Parlement of Paris and the Fronde, 1643–1652.* Princeton, 1971.   77
———. "The French Crown versus Its Judicial and Financial Officials," *Journal of Modern History,* XXXIV (1962), 146–60.   77
Mousnier, R. *Fureurs paysannes.* Paris, 1967.   81
*———. *Peasant Uprisings in Seventeenth-Century France, Russia, and China.* English translation. New York, 1972.
———. *Les Hiérarchies sociales de 1450 à nos jours.* Paris, 1969.
———. *Social Hierarchies, 1450 to the Present.* English translation. New York, 1973.
———. *Les Institutions de la France sous la monarchie absolue,* Vol. I. Paris, 1974.   74, 80
———. *La Plume, la faucille et le marteau* [collected essays]. Paris, 1970.   71, 93
———. *Les XVIe et XVIIe siècles.* Paris, 1954.   73
———, ed. *Le Conseil du roi, de Louis XII à la Révolution.* Paris, 1970.   74, 80
———, ed. *Lettres et mémoires adressés au chancelier Séguier (1633–1649).* 2 vols. Paris, 1964.   80
———. *La Dîme de Vauban.* Paris, Centre de Documentation Universitaire, 1969.   93
———. *État et société en France aux XVIIe et XVIIIe siècles.* Paris, Centre de Documentation Universitaire, 1969.
———. *État et société sous François Ier et pendant le gouvernement personnel de Louis XIV,* Parts I, II. Paris, Centre de Documentation Universitaire, 1967.   80
Neveu, B., ed. *Acta nuntiaturae gallicae: Correspondance du nonce en France Angelo Ranuzzi (1683–1689).* 2 vols. Rome, 1973.   82
New Cambridge Modern History, Vols. 5, 6. Cambridge, 1961, 1970.   86, 89, 92
Noailles, Duc de. *Histoire de Madame de Maintenon et des principaux événements du règne de Louis XIV.* 4 vols. Paris, 1849–58.   40
*Ogg, D. *Louis XIV.* London, 1933.   56
Olivier-Martin, F. *Histoire du droit français.* Paris, 1948.   71
———. *L'Organisation corporative de la France d'ancien régime.* Paris, 1938.   79

————. *L'Absolutisme monarchique* (Cours doctorat, Faculté de Droit).
    Paris, 1950.   **65**
————. *Le Conseil d'état du roi* (Cours doctorat, Faculté de Droit). Paris,
    1947.
————. *Les Lois du roi au XVII⁰ et XVIII⁰ siècle* (Cours doctorat, Faculté
    de Droit). Paris, 1945.
Orcibal, J. *Louis XIV contre Innocent XI.* Paris, 1949.   **82**
————. *Louis XIV et les protestants.* Paris, 1951.   **83**
Pagès, G. *Le Grand Electeur et Louis XIV: 1660–1688.* Paris, 1905.   **43**
————. *La Monarchie d'ancien régime en France (de Henri IV à Louis XIV).*
    Paris, 1928.   **56**
————. "Le Gouvernement et l'administration monarchiques en France à la
    fin du règne de Louis XIV," *Revue des cours et conférences,* XXXVIII
    (1936–37), 1–9, 289–98, 610–19, 703–12.   **64**
————. *Les Origines du XVIII⁰ siècle au temps de Louis XIV (1680–1715).*
    Paris, Centre de Documentation Universitaire, 1961.   **64**
Pellisson, P. *Histoire de Louis XIV.* 3 vols. Paris, 1749.   **14**
Picavet, C. G. *La Diplomatie française au temps de Louis XIV.* Paris, 1930.
    65
Préclin, E., and E. Jarry. *Les Luttes politiques et doctrinales aux XVII⁰ et
    XVIII⁰ siècles,* Vol. 19¹ of Fliche and Martin, *Histoire de l'église.*
    Paris, 1955.
"Problèmes de politique étrangère sous Louis XIV" [essays by V.-L. Tapié,
    G. Livet, A.-J. Bourde, J. Meuvret], in *XVII⁰ Siècle,* Nos. 46–47
    (1960).   **86, 87**
Puaux, F. "Origines, causes et conséquences de la guerre des camisards,"
    Revue historique, CXXIX (1918), 1–21.   **44**
Puaux, F., and A. Sabatier. *Études sur la révocation de l'édit de Nantes.*
    Paris, 1886.   **44**
Ranke, L. von. *Französische Geschichte, vornehmlich im sechzehnten und
    siebzehnten Jahrhundert.* 5 vols. Stuttgart, 1856–62.   **33**
°Ranum, O. *Paris in the Age of Absolutism.* New York, 1968.   **69**
Ravaisson, F., ed. *Archives de la Bastille.* 16 vols. Paris, 1866–84.   **42**
*Recueil des instructions données aux ambassadeurs et ministres de France
    depuis les traités de Westphalie jusqu'à la révolution française.* 29
    vols. Paris, 1884–1969.   **85**
Rich, E. E., and C. H. Wilson, eds. *The Cambridge Economic History of
    Europe,* Vol. IV: *The Economy of Expanding Europe in the Sixteenth
    and Seventeenth Centuries.* Cambridge, 1967.
Richet, D. *La France moderne: L'Esprit des institutions.* Paris, 1973.
Robert, D. "Louis XIV et les protestants," *XVII⁰ Siècle,* Nos. 76–77
    (1967), 39–52.   **84**
Rothkrug, L. *Opposition to Louis XIV: The Political and Social Origins of
    the French Enlightenment.* Princeton, 1965.   **93**
Rousset, C. *Histoire de Louvois.* 4 vols. Paris, 1861–63.   **42**
Rowen, H. H. *The Ambassador Prepares for War: The Dutch Embassy of
    Arnauld de Pomponne, 1669–1671.* The Hague, 1957.   **88**
————. " 'L'État c'est à moi': Louis XIV and the State," *French Historical
    Studies,* II (1961), 83–98.   **71, 72**
Rule, J. C., ed. *Louis XIV and the Craft of Kingship.* Columbus, Ohio,
    1969.   **69, 77, 83, 85, 88, 90**
Sagnac, P. *La Formation de la société française moderne,* Vol. I: *1661–
    1715.* Paris, 1945.   **79**

Sagnac, P., and A. de Saint-Léger. *La Prépondérance française: Louis XIV (1661–1715)*. Paris, 1935.   56
Sainte-Beuve, C. A. *Port-Royal*. 5 vols. Paris, 1840–59.   43
Saint-Germain, J. *Les Financiers sous Louis XIV: Paul Poisson de Bourvalais*. Paris, 1950.   92
———. *La Reynie et la police au grand siècle*. Paris, 1962.   76
———. *Louis XIV secret*. Paris, 1970.   69
———. *Samuel Bernard, le banquier des rois*. Paris, 1960.   92
Saint-Pierre, Abbé de. *Annales politiques*. 2 vols. London, 1757.   14
Saint-Simon, Duc de, *Mémoires*, A. de Boislisle, ed. 43 vols. Paris, 1879–1930.   39
———. *Parallèle des trois premiers rois Bourbons*, in Faugère, ed., *Écrits inédits de Saint-Simon*, Vol. I. Paris, 1880.   45
Salmon, J. H. M. "Venality of Office and Popular Sedition in Seventeenth-Century France," *Past and Present*, No. 37 (1967), 21–43.   81
Schmittlein, R. *L'Aspect politique du différend Bossuet-Fénelon*. Paris, 1954.   83
Scoville, W. C. *The Persecution of the Huguenots and French Economic Development: 1680–1720*. Berkeley, 1960.   84
Sée, H. *Histoire économique de la France: Le Moyen Âge et l'ancien régime*. Paris, 1939.   62
———. "Que faut-il penser de l'œuvre économique de Colbert?" *Revue historique*, CLIII (1926), 181–94.   61
"Serviteurs du roi. Quelques Aspects de la fonction publique dans la société française du XVII⁰ siècle," in *XVII⁰ Siècle*, Nos. 42–43 (1959).   80
Shennan, J. H. *The Parlement of Paris*. Ithaca, N.Y., 1968.
Sismondi. S. de. *Histoire des français*. 31 vols. Paris, 1821–44.   31
Sonnino, P. "The Dating and Authorship of Louis XIV's *Mémoires*," *French Historical Studies*, III (1964), 303–37.   70
———. *Louis XIV's View of the Papacy (1661–1667)*. Berkeley, 1966.   82
———, ed. and translator. *Mémoires for the Instruction of the Dauphin, by Louis XIV*. New York, 1970.   70
Sources, Marquis de. *Mémoires*, de Cosnac *et al.*, eds. 13 vols. Paris, 1882–93.   39, 45
Srbik, H. R. von. *Wien und Versailles, 1692–1697*. Munich, 1944.   85
Tapié, V.-L. "Europe et chrétienté. Idée chrétienne et gloire dynastique dans la politique européenne au moment du siège de Vienne (1683)," *Gregorianum*, XLII (1961), 268–89.   87
Taveneaux, R., ed. *Jansénisme et politique*. Paris, 1965.   83
Thireau, J.-L. *Les Idées politiques de Louis XIV*. Paris, 1973.   71
Thomas, J.-F. *La Querelle de l'Unigenitus*. Paris, 1950.   83
Treca, G. *Les Doctrines et les réformes de droit public en réaction contre l'absolutisme de Louis XIV dans l'entourage du duc de Bourgogne*. Paris, 1909.   45
Trevor-Roper, H. R. "Fernand Braudel, the *Annales*, and the Mediterranean," *Journal of Modern History*, XLIV (1972), 468–79.   95
Vast, H., ed. *Les Grands Traités du règne de Louis XIV*. 3 vols. Paris, 1893–99.   43
Vauban. *Projet d'une dîme royale*, E. Daire, ed. Paris, 1843.   45
Voltaire. *Essai sur les mœurs et l'esprit des nations*. Paris, 1756.   15
———. *Le Siècle de Louis XIV*. Berlin, 1751.   15
°———. *The Age of Louis XIV*. English translation. London, 1961.

Weiss, C. *Histoire des réfugiés protestants de France depuis la révocation de l'édit de Nantes jusqu'à nos jours.* 2 vols. Paris, 1853.   **44**

———. *History of the French Protestant Refugees, from the Revocation of the Edict of Nantes to Our Own Days.* 2 vols., English translation. New York, 1854.

*Wolf, J. B. *The Emergence of the Great Powers, 1685–1715.* New York, 1951.

*———. *Louis XIV.* New York, 1968.   **68**

———. "The Reign of Louis XIV: A Selected Bibliography of Writings since the War of 1914–1918," *Journal of Modern History,* XXXVI (1964), 127–44.

Zeller, G. *Aspects de la politique française sous l'ancien régime* [collected essays]. Paris, 1964.   **66**

———. *Histoire des relations internationales,* Vol. III²: *De Louis XIV à 1789.* Paris, 1955.   **85**

———. "La Monarchie d'ancien régime et les frontières naturelles," *Revue d'histoire moderne,* VIII (1933), 305–33.   **66**

———. "Politique extérieure et diplomatie sous Louis XIV," *Revue d'histoire moderne,* VI (1931), 124–43.   **66**

Ziegler, G. *Les Coulisses de Versailles,* Vol. I: *Le Règne de Louis XIV.* Paris, 1963.   **69**

Index